THE STRATEGIC GUIDE TO SHAPING
YOUR STUDENT AFFAIRS CAREER

THE STRATEGIC GUIDE TO SHAPING YOUR STUDENT AFFAIRS CAREER

Sonja Ardoin

Foreword by Marcia B. Baxter Magolda

STERLING, VIRGINIA

Published by Stylus Publishing, LLC.
22883 Quicksilver Drive
Sterling, Virginia 20166-2102

Library of Congress Cataloging-in-Publication Data
Ardoin, Sonja.
The strategic guide to shaping your student affairs career /
Sonja Ardoin.
    pages cm
Includes bibliographical references and index.
ISBN 978-1-57922-958-0 (pbk. : alk. paper)
ISBN 978-1-57922-957-3 (cloth : alk. paper)
ISBN 978-1-57922-959-7 (library networkable e-edition)
ISBN 978-1-57922-960-3 (consumer e-edition)
1. Student counselors—Vocational guidance—United States.
2. Student affairs services—United States. I. Title.
LB2343.A74 2014
378.1'97—dc23

                                                    2013044434

13-digit ISBN: 978-1-57922-957-3 (cloth)
13-digit ISBN: 978-1-57922-958-0 (paperback)
13-digit ISBN: 978-1-57922-959-7 (library networkable e-edition)
13-digit ISBN: 978-1-57922-960-3 (consumer e-edition)

Printed in the United States of America

All first editions printed on acid-free paper
that meets the American National Standards Institute
Z39-48 Standard.

Bulk Purchases

Quantity discounts are available for use in workshops and for
staff development.
Call 1-800-232-0223

First Edition, 2014

10   9   8

To anyone who has broken boundaries or statistics in obtaining an education, who has opened the door for others, or who has sacrificed for his or her children to have the opportunity. You have changed lives. Thank you.

I know this achievement is not mine alone; rather, it is a collective effort of everyone who has participated in my life. I am forever indebted.

CONTENTS

FOREWORD

Marcia B. Baxter Magolda

A key challenge of navigating adult life is finding one's purpose. This is a far more complex task than choosing a college major, mastering content knowledge, building skills, and attending graduate school or acquiring a job. It involves finding your own way into adulthood by recomposing the meaning others have made for you during childhood and adolescence. A central part of this process is coming to know yourself—what you believe and value, how you make sense of your identity, and how you craft adult relationships. Emerging adulthood is a time to re-evaluate the external messages you have received about what to believe, how to identify, and how to relate to others to develop your own internal criteria for making meaning of these parts of yourself. This capacity to self-author your beliefs, identity, and relationships provides a compass to navigate the complex work and personal roles you find yourself in as an adult. As you encounter conflicting expectations, multiple perspectives on what is ethical, the need to interact with others who see things differently than you do, and ambiguity about how to proceed, you can turn to your internal compass for guidance.

Developing self-authorship, or an internal compass, is a difficult process. It requires thoughtful reflection on your experiences, recognition that you can only control your reaction to what happens to you, and intentional attention to sorting out your reactions to the complexity of everyday life and work. This process is facilitated when those around you frame learning opportunities around your experiences, respect your feelings and thoughts, and engage collaboratively with you as you sort out your own thoughts and feelings. When you are invited to consider the complexity of your work and life decisions, bring your personal authority to these decisions, and work interdependently with others you have the opportunity to develop self-authorship. Self-authoring your early adult life is a joint journey—one in which you direct the journey by recomposing your meaning internally and one that requires support from others for your new ways of constructing your world. You are in the captain's seat on the front of a tandem bicycle, directing the journey. But you need good learning partners, or good company, on the back seat to provide guidance and help you balance as you make life decisions. This is the kind of good company the student affairs profession advocates providing for collegians. And it is the kind of good company Sonja Ardoin and her colleagues provide for emerging and continuing student affairs professionals in this book.

Ardoin and her coauthors invite readers into a learning partnership to navigate becoming a student affairs educator. She begins by introducing the complexity of higher education, the role of student affairs in educating diverse students, the multiple ways in which institutional type and student affairs organizational structures shape functional areas, and nuances of graduate preparation programs to prepare for student affairs work. More important, Ardoin moves quickly into encouraging readers to reflect on how their values fit with those of the profession and how their skills correlate with those required for success. This emphasis on bringing one's personal authority to career planning is a central theme of the book. Ardoin advocates professionals taking responsibility for their own growth and development and approaching their careers with intentionality. To assist readers in taking up the invitation, she provides a concrete career strategy that includes five components: lifelong learning, extending your experiences, planning for professional development, networking and connecting, and self-reflection. The book explicitly addresses balancing intentionality and flexibility in advocating these strategies as processes for continued growth. Ardoin emphasizes personal authority in her focus on developing one's individual style for how to plan, strategize, network, and reflect. She recognizes that career planning is not a one-size-fits-all process and provides good questions, worksheets, and resources throughout to help focus self-reflection, assessment, and personal stock-taking. In doing so she conveys the value of readers' thoughts, feelings, and voices.

Ardoin clearly portrays readers' experiences as opportunities for learning and growth. She and her contributors, whose personal stories appear throughout the book, demonstrate how to engage in lifelong learning and how to build on professional experiences over the course of one's career. In doing so they illustrate the crucial role building relationships with colleagues plays in developing a meaningful work life. Ardoin explicitly recognizes the value of all constituents in her discussion of building relationships, asking readers not to be "too good" to interact with young professionals who have insight into the latest literature and student culture. She advocates connecting with custodial staff and cashiers who all make contributions to the campus community and are sources for learning. This sense of working interdependently to create healthy learning environments for collegians and educators promotes self-authorship.

Good learning partners share their experience authentically, acknowledge their mistakes, and reveal how they recompose meaning as a result of difficult experiences. Yet they do not impose their meaning making on others. Ardoin and her colleagues offer their diverse stories here authentically, opening windows into the process of navigating adult life and work. They model self-reflection and reveal not only how they implement the strategies but their personal pathways and insights. They are careful to remind readers that these are their experiences and that readers might feel differently. The emphasis on finding one's own voice to bring to navigating one's career permeates the book.

Student affairs educators advocate intentional learning for collegians, encouraging them to reflect on their experiences; develop their own beliefs, values, and identities to guide their life decisions; and take responsibility for their educational and life journeys. In order to create intentional learning environments that promote self-authorship, student affairs educators also need to be intentional learners who can reflect on skills and abilities to identify areas for continued growth; reflect on and establish internal beliefs, identities, and social relations; and take responsibility for continued professional growth. The complexities of developing self-authorship, for both collegians and educators, warrants as much good company as possible. Ardoin and her colleagues offer good company for readers in various stages of student affairs careers to recompose meaningful work and adult lives.

ACKNOWLEDGMENTS

I would like to express my heartfelt appreciation for and give recognition to the following people:

- My parents, Evelyn and Steve Ardoin, for their continuous support and sacrifice to help get me where I am today
- My grandparents, Dorothy and Lennis Guillory and Grace and Polly Ardoin, for their example of work ethic and the foundation they set from which we could all build
- My godchildren, Tyler and Morgan Guillory and Julia Downs, for making me want to be a good role model and for reminding me to set the stage for those who will come after me
- My friends, whom I also call my chosen family—Bridget Ardoin Fuselier, Koren Smith, Allison Brown Scalia, Sara Rider Schulz, Chloe Wiley, Jesse Gomez Downs, Steven Scales, Lindsey Katherine Dippold, and David Pittman—for their listening ears, constant support, and laughter and for helping me find ways to balance my life
- The contributing writers for this book (see p. 163 for their bios), all of whom are gracious friends and colleagues, for their willingness to share their stories to allow others to learn and their belief that this project was worthy of their time and talents
- John von Knorring and the entire Stylus Publishing staff for presenting an opportunity I never thought possible, being patient as I tried to write a dissertation and book in the same year, and supporting me throughout the process as a first-time book author
- Dr. K. C. White, who directed me to the field of higher education
- Jesse Gomez Downs, who was my first comrade in this work and is still one of my favorites
- Dr. Robert Schwartz, Jackie Thomas Jr., David Pittman, Dr. Adam Sterritt, Dani Su Bickley, Ryan O'Connell, Crystal Sutton, Keith Echols, Elizabeth Flash, Dr. Mary Coburn, Vicki Dobiyanski, Rusty Thompson, merz lim, Neil Schaffer, Dr. Audrey Jaeger, Jeremy Tuchmayer, Dr. Matt Gregory, Dr. Mike Walker, Jaime Russell, Sarah

Teitelbaum, Stefanie Mancuso, and Larry Wray, all of whom I have had the good fortune to work with directly at one point or another in my career

- My higher education colleagues throughout the years from Louisiana State University, Florida State University, Texas A&M University, North Carolina State University, the University of North Carolina Wilmington, Mortar Board National Senior Honor Society, LeaderShape, Inc., Zeta Tau Alpha, Lambda Chi Alpha, the Social Justice Training Institute, and many other institutions and organizations, for their commitment to teaching and learning, for their desire to increase knowledge and access, for supporting people's growth and development, for being champions for social justice, and for contributing to my professional and personal development

- My K–12 teachers and higher education professors for seeing my potential, cultivating my abilities, and pushing me beyond what the statistics said I could achieve

INTRODUCTION TO
THE FIELD

Higher education, and particularly student affairs, is not typically a career field a person dreams of pursuing during childhood. It would probably be shocking to hear a child exclaim, "I want to be a residence director . . . or dean of students . . . or vice president for student affairs when I grow up!" Children probably cannot conceive of this option, unless their parents have held similar roles. In fact, many people do not realize the field exists until they are actually on a college campus as an undergraduate student. Even then, undergraduate students may not recognize the options of higher education careers unless they are involved with campus student affairs functions or an administrator or faculty member directs them to explore the field.

The majority of student affairs educators have similar stories about how they found their way into the field. The story goes something like this: "I was a student involved on campus [in residence halls, in fraternity or sorority life, in student government, on a programming board, in multicultural affairs, on a conduct board, in campus recreation, etc.] and [insert person's name] told me one day that I could continue that kind of work as an actual career after college. I had never thought of that and decided to see what it was all about."

Because the typical path into the field is through undergraduate involvement and conversations with, or mentoring from, current student affairs educators, it is crucial that we understand who the students on our campuses are and how we can encourage a diverse array of people to give consideration to the field of higher education and student affairs.

Student Demographics on Today's College Campuses

Higher education has come a long way from its roots as an all-male, all-White, wealthy, and religiously affiliated endeavor. In fact, student bodies on many of today's campuses rarely reflect the history of higher education. This is, in part, due to the changing demographics in U.S. high schools. As both a *Chronicle of Higher Education* blog post and a Lawlor Group report mentioned in June 2013, "High-school populations are becoming more diverse, and more and more prospective [college] applicants are low-income and first-generation students" (Hoover, 2013, p. 1; Lawlor Group, 2013). College students are representing a wider variety of races and ethnicities, including biracial and multiracial students, and higher education admissions officers are now encouraging institutions to create recruitment and admissions publications and web content in Spanish and other languages (Hoover, 2013). Along with considering students' race and ethnicity, socioeconomic status, and whether they are first generation, colleges and universities are hosting more students with a variety of sexual orientations, religious affiliations, ages, mental and physical ability levels, military statuses, and partner and caretaker roles.

Despite the increasing diversity of students enrolling in colleges and universities, higher education is not necessarily seeing the same representation in its graduates. Rather, higher education tends to repeat history in who achieves degree completion. The American Council on Education (ACE) published a report in May 2013 that revealed "individuals who earned their baccalaureate degrees in 2007–2008 were not nearly as racially diverse as the overall undergraduate student body. They were largely unmarried, childless, white young adults in their early 20s who were financially dependent on their parents and who seamlessly moved along the path toward degree attainment" (ACE Report, 2013, p. 1). The statistic ACE reports further demonstrate this disparity: "Whites represented three out of every four students completing a bachelor's degree. Students tended to be young (an average age of 18.7 at the time of college entry) and to have graduated within five years, with Asian Americans and whites more likely to be the traditional age than other minority groups. Most graduates also came from upper or middle-class family backgrounds, and 58 percent were women" (2013, p. 2). The only change from higher education's history, it seems, is that more females are both accessing and completing college degrees than males.

Although today's college student populations may be more diverse in both visible and invisible ways, it is concerning that graduates from institutions are not representing that diversity. Furthermore, if we must possess a bachelor's degree and, in many cases, a master's degree in order to seek a career as a student affairs educator, the field will never be as representative of the students we work with if we cannot graduate more diverse students.

Have our colleges and universities really become more holistically accessible and inclusive, or are institutions allowing new populations of students to access higher education without providing them with the necessary resources and support to retain and persist to graduation? This question begs another: Can the role of student affairs on campus fill the gap between enrollment and graduation for today's new college students?

The Role of Student Affairs on Campus

Student affairs fundamentally concentrates on the growth and development of students outside of the classroom environment. We know that student affairs educators also partake in curriculum creation and implementation for some credit-bearing courses, serve on committees to develop university policy and procedure, act as central figures in university risk and crisis management, and supply a host of other contributions. The purpose of student affairs is to work collaboratively with academic affairs to create a seamless learning environment for students that allows them to explore their career options and gain intellectual and life skills in order to contribute to their current and future communities and society at large. Many college and university mission statements refer to "developing the whole student," and the role of student affairs is central to that type of mission.

The role of student affairs has been altered and shifted throughout the history of higher education. Fenske (1989) aptly described the evolution of the field: "[Student affairs] has never had a single functional focus, has never been stable in its role over significant periods of time, and has never had a consensual integrative philosophy" (p. 27). The role of student affairs varies from campus to campus. A functional area that may fall under student affairs tutelage at one institution is slated as an academic affairs responsibility at another institution. Variations tend to depend on how institutions are structured and what areas are coupled together.

Student Affairs by Institutional Type

Colleges and universities are designated by institutional type based on characteristics including but not limited to size, funding, degrees offered, institutional missions, and student demographics. Descriptions in size include large (over 10,000), midsize (3,000–9,999), small (1,000–2,999), and very small (under 1,000). Most institutions have a mixture of funding; however, they are separated into the two categories of public and private by their primary method of funding or their historical method of funding, which is why some state institutions are now called "state supported" rather than "state funded." Degree offerings provide another institutional type category, splitting schools into associate colleges, baccalaureate colleges, master's colleges and universities, doctorate-granting universities, special-focus institutions (law schools, medical schools, Bible colleges, etc.), and tribal colleges. The student populations that dominate colleges and universities further separate institutions into types, which include predominantly White institutions (PWIs); historically Black colleges and universities (HBCUs); Hispanic-serving institutions (HSIs); Asian American, Native American, and Pacific Islander–serving institutions (AANAPISIs); men's colleges; and women's colleges.

As you can imagine, there are quite a number of possible combinations for institutional type designations. You can have a large, public, doctoral-granting PWI; a small, private, baccalaureate HSI; or a midsize, public, master's HBCU. The list could go on and on. The good news for student affairs educators is that all of these various institutional types need people to help facilitate their student affairs divisions.

Although the role of student affairs is relatively similar at all colleges and universities, there are some differences in how student affairs functions at each institutional type. Larger universities will typically have larger divisions of student affairs that need student affairs educators to be more specific in their roles, serving in only one major functional area. Smaller colleges will, similarly, have smaller divisions of student affairs that require student affairs educators to be more general in their skill sets and willing to serve in multiple functional areas or at least be open to frequent collaboration—in every sense of the word. In addition, HBCUs, HSIs, AANAPISIs, men's colleges, and women's colleges often seek student affairs educators who either share identities with or have an understanding of the student populations most often served by those institutions.

Institutional type may influence whether you are interested in working at certain colleges and universities or whether you are qualified to do so. It is key to recognize that institutional type can have an impact on career path. Experiences at large institutions tend to shape you as more of a specialist, whereas smaller institutions can provide you with more generalist skill sets. As you progress through graduate programs and the beginning of your career, it is important to consider whether you desire to gain experiences at a variety of institutional types. Try to utilize internships, practica, or volunteering to gain hands-on encounters at different kinds of colleges and universities to better determine what type of institution(s) best suits you and to broaden your skill sets and résumé. It may also be helpful to review books such as *Where You Work Matters* by Joan Hirt (2006); these books discuss at length how institutional type combines with student affairs to create unique experiences for student affairs educators and can help you understand how student affairs functions at these institutions without your having to physically visit each type.

Student Affairs Structures

Although the specifics of student affairs structures vary based on institutional type and individual institution, the two primary frameworks for student affairs structures either have student affairs as a stand-alone division or join student affairs with academic affairs as one division.

Student Affairs as Its Own Division

Around the United States, a host of institutions choose to combine their student affairs areas into their own division, often titled Division of Student Affairs or Division of Student Life. The units that compose the division vary and may or may not include other areas such as enrollment management. Examples of a single student affairs structure can be seen from Colorado State University, Florida A&M University, Florida International University, and Miami University of Ohio (see Figures 1.1, 1.2, 1.3, and 1.4).

Student Affairs Combined With Academic Affairs

Since the economic downturn in the United States, colleges and universities have been receiving fewer financial contributions from state governments, private donors, and/or institutional endowments. This financial situation has encouraged many institutions to critically examine their structures. Some institutions have decided that coupling student affairs with academic affairs may ease the financial strain at the institution and encourage further collaboration between student affairs and academic affairs functions. Thus, they have created Divisions of Academic and Student Affairs. Examples of a combined structure can be seen from North Carolina State University, Portland Community College, Tulane University, and the University of New Mexico (see Figures 1.5, 1.6, 1.7, and 1.8).

Regardless of overall division structure, student affairs tends to house certain functional units within colleges and universities. The next section will briefly discuss each of these functional units.

Functional Areas

Student affairs is an umbrella term for a variety of functional units within higher education institutions. These units tend to assist students with learning and growth opportunities outside of the classroom environment. Divisions of student affairs characteristically encompass many of the following units: academic advising, accountability and advocacy, admissions, alumni affairs, assessment and professional development, campus ministries, career services,

Figure 1.1 Colorado State University. This institution is considered a large, public, doctoral-granting PWI. Adapted with permission from www.studentaffairs.colostate.edu/Data/Sites/1/documents/staff/locations/vpsa-org-chart.pdf.

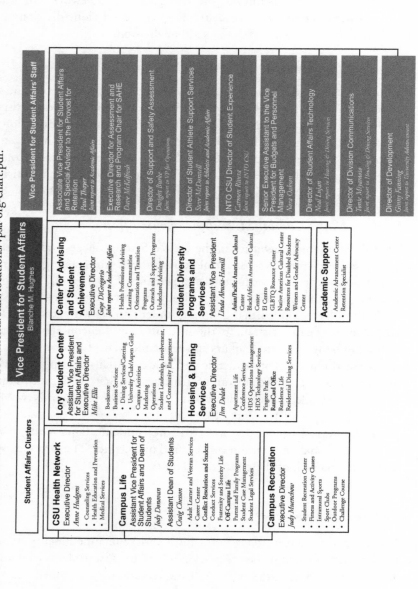

Figure 1.1 (cont.)

THE DIVISION OF STUDENT AFFAIRS	
Department	**Services**
Office of the Vice President for Student Affairs:	Coordinates programs and services to support students in and out of the classroom.
Parent and Family Programs	Provides programs and services to parents and families of current CSU students.
Retention Coordinator	Provides academic coaching and support to students for Denver Scholarship Foundation.
Student Affairs in Higher Education Graduate Program M.S.	Graduate program for those seeking careers in student development at the higher education level.
Support and Safety Assessment	Provides services to assist CSU students and employees with health, well-being or safety concerns.
Academic Advancement Center	Provides services to help low-income, first-generation college students, foster youth, and students with disabilities to stay in college.
Adult Learner and Veteran Services	Provides programs and services focused on adult learners including student parents and student veterans, with the goal to persist to graduation.
Campus Recreation	Provides a variety of wellness and healthy lifestyle opportunities in the following programs: Intramural Sports, Sport Clubs, Fitness & Mind-Body Classes, Massage Therapy, Outdoor Programs, and Challenge Ropes Course.
Career Center	Supports students in their career goalsCenter for Advising and Student Achievement (CASA)Provides a wide range of programs and services focused on transitions, advising, retention, and student success.
Center for Advising and Student Achievement:	Provides a wide range of programs and services focused on transitions, advising, retention, and student success.
Learning Communities	The Key Communities (Key Academic Community, Key Service Community, Key Explore Community, Key Health Professions Community, and Key Plus Community) are diverse first- and second-year learning communities designed to assist students with their transition to and through the university.
Health Professions Advising	Provides pre-professional advising to current students and alumi who are pursuing a career in any of the human or animal health professions.
Undeclared Advising	Provides academic advising for undeclared students and those interested in exploring majors.
Orientation and Transition Programs	Serving first-year, second-year and transfer students with programs including CSU Connect Orientation, Preview First-year Orientation, Next Step Transfer Orientation, Preview Mountain Experience, Ram Welcome, First Year Mentoring Program, Transfer Mentoring, Transfer Interest Groups, Getting To Year 2 at CSU Conference, Year 2 Programs.
Outreach and Support	Offers mentoring and support for students in selected scholarship programs as well as strategic interventions to increase retention and graduation.
Conflict Resolution and Student Conduct Services	Provides mediation services and holds students accountable for policy violations.
CSU Health Network:	
Medical Services	Promotes complete physical and mental health by providing quality health care and comprehensive health education to enhance all aspects of a student's well-being.
Counseling Services	
Health Education and Prevention Services	
Fraternity and Sorority Life	Supports fraternity and sorority life.
Housing and Dining Services:	
Apartment Life	Provides a community environment that is both socially and academically enriching with single and family apartments.
Conference Services	Assists more than 100 programs each year ranging in size from under 10 to more than 7,000 participants.
Dining Services	Six dining centers offer chef-created, global cuisine and modern conveniences. Flexible dining options such as to-go meals, online ordering, and late-night dining are also available.
Pingree Park Mountain Campus	Beautiful CSU mountain campus available for conferences, workshops, retreats, and team-building activities.
RamCard	Produces identification cards and staff badges, manages vending contracts and services, and administers the RamCash program for the university.
Residence Life	Includes 13 residence halls housing more than 5,000 students in safe and inclusive learning environments.
Lory Student Center:	Great place to eat, shop, meet friends, have bikes repaired, hang out, or study in one of the many Student Center lounges.
Campus Activities	A great place to learn about the many exciting outside-the-classroom possibilities and volunteer opportunities available to students.
ASAP (Student Activities Board)	Student-led group that selects and brings comedians, performers, speakers, films, and other entertainment to campus.
CSU Bookstore	Offers textbooks, school & art supplies, backpacks, CSU logo clothing, and gifts.
Dining Services	Provides eating and dining services. Flexible hours and variety lets everyone enjoy something they like.
Off-Campus Life	Supports students living in the Fort Collins community.
Student Leadership, Involvement, & Community Engagement	Provides programs and services to student organizations, student leaders and student volunteers to enrich their academic and social experience at CSU.
Student Organizations	Provides programs and services to student organizations.
Student Legal Services	Provides legal assistance to students.
Student Case Management	Connects students with medical, mental health, personal or family crisis, illness, or injury to appropriate campus and community resources.
Student Diversity Programs and Services:	
Asian/Pacific American Cultural Center	
Black/African American Cultural Center	
El Centro	CSU is proud of its efforts to enhance, appreciate, and support diversity and multiculturalism. These offices are designed to support students in a variety of ways and provide opportunities to successfully participate in, and contribute to, the diverse campus environment. While each office listed may emphasize a specific segment of the student body, services and programs are available to benefit all students of CSU.
Gay, Lesbian, Bisexual, Transgender, Queer, Questioning, and Ally Resorce Center	
Native American Cultural Center	
Resources for Disabled Students	
Women and Gender Advocacy Center	

Figure 1.2 Florida A&M University. This institution is considered a large, public, doctoral-granting HBCU. Adapted from www.famu.edu/StudentLife/Student%620Life%205_13%20B.pdf.

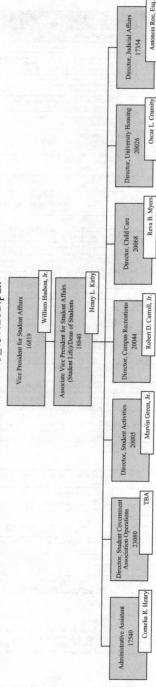

Figure 1.3 Florida International University. This institution is considered a large, public, doctoral-granting HSI. Reproduced with permission from http://studentaffairs.fiu.edu/wp-content/uploads/2013/01/SAchart.pdf.

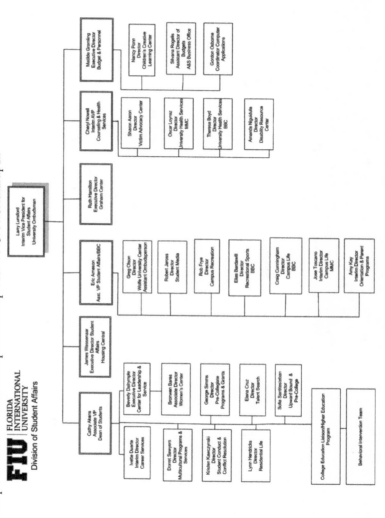

Figure 1.4 Miami University of Ohio. This institution is considered a large, public, doctoral-granting PWI. Reproduced with permission from www.units.miamioh.edu/saf/PDF/OrgChart.pdf.

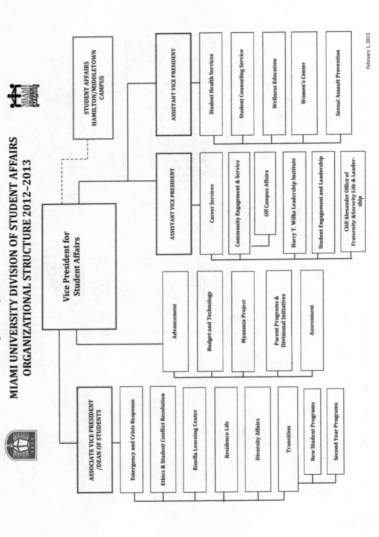

MIAMI UNIVERSITY DIVISION OF STUDENT AFFAIRS
ORGANIZATIONAL STRUCTURE 2012–2013

Figure 1.5 North Carolina State University. This institution is considered a large, public, doctoral-granting PWI. Reproduced with permission from http://dasa.ncsu.edu/sites/default/files/orgcharts/dasa.pdf

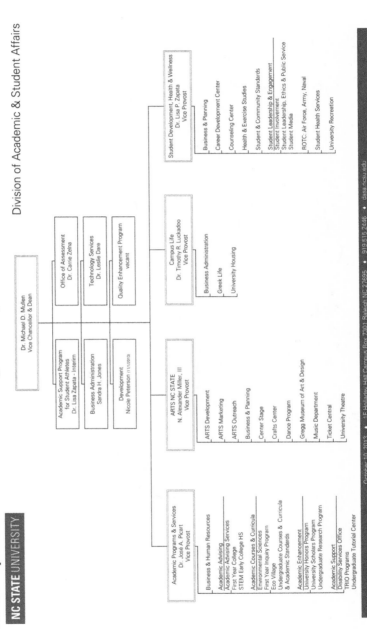

Figure 1.6 Portland Community College. This institution is considered a large, public, associate college PWI. Reproduced with permission from www.pcc.edu/ir/OrgChart/201314/201314acad.pdf

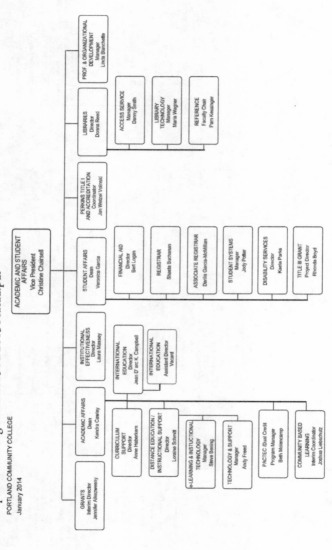

Figure 1.7 Tulane University. This institution is considered a large, private, doctoral-granting PWI. Adapted with permission from http://tulane.edu/provost/upload/ChartOrganization070113.pdf.

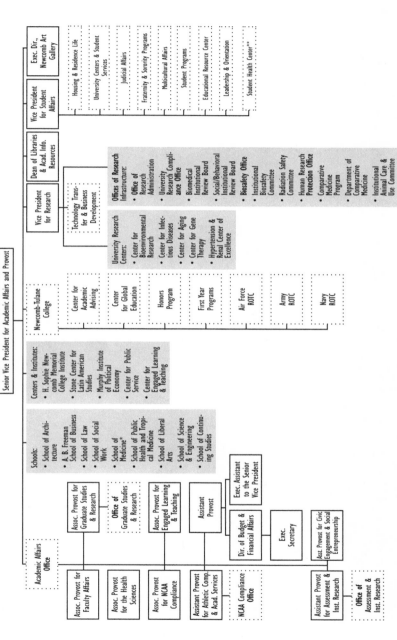

* The Dean of Medicine reports to the Sr. Vice President for Academic Affairs and Provost for academic appointments
** On clinical issues, the Student Health Center reports to the Dean of Medicine.

Figure 1.8 University of New Mexico. This institution is considered a large, public, doctoral-granting HSI. Reproduced with permission from http://studentaffairs.unm.edu/osa_org_chart_8_2013.pdf

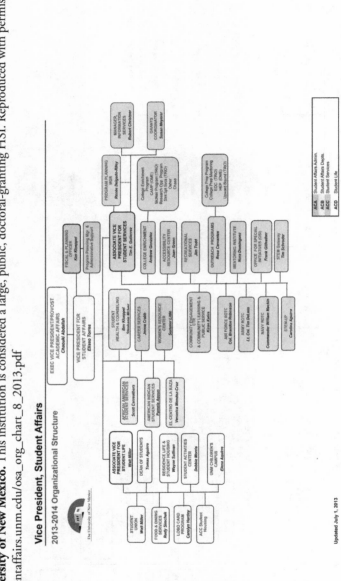

development and fund-raising, fraternity and sorority life, health and wellness or campus recreation, human resources, information technology, leadership and service, orientation and the first-year experience, residence life, student activities and student unions, study abroad, and areas designed to assist underrepresented student populations such as offices and centers of multicultural affairs, LGBTQ (lesbian, gay, bisexual, transgender, and questioning/queer), women, veterans' affairs, "nontraditional" students, and more. As one can see, student affairs educators serve students in a variety of ways; they assist students in making transitions into and out of college, provide students with places to call home, create opportunities for students to attain academic and life skills, and help students maintain health and wellness. These educators help students grow and develop mentally, emotionally, physically, and spiritually—a concentration on the whole student. Each of these student affairs areas gives attention to an aspect that is important to the overall collegiate experience and to the successful retention and persistence of students.

Academic Advising

Academic advising involves assisting students in making their course selections and registering, understanding and meeting their degree requirements, and completing all necessary obligations for graduation. These advisors are great sources of academic information for students and often refer students to other campus resources. Academic advisors also sometimes teach academic courses.

Accountability (or Student Conduct) and Advocacy

Offices of accountability and advocacy promote and maintain conduct codes and ensure that campus community members are living by those codes and creating a safe and healthy environment for themselves and others. These offices are the first point of contact for students in any kind of distress or people who are highly concerned about the well-being of others. They also teach better decision-making strategies and handle adjudication of any conduct code violations.

Admissions

Admissions, or recruitment, offices seek to promote the university to prospective students and families. Professionals from these offices visit high schools, host on-campus guests, and guide students through the details of the university admissions process. Admissions offices also collect information that contributes to the overall enrollment management and retention goals of the institution.

Alumni Affairs

Alumni affairs, engagement, or association offices foster continued engagement with alumni of the institution. They host events to bring people back to campus and to allow alumni who have moved away to connect with one another in other cities. Alumni affairs tends to work closely with the development office when alumni are interested in giving their time, talent, or treasure back to the institution.

Assessment and Professional Development

Assessment and professional development areas tend to focus more internally on student affairs departments and staff. They assist the Division of Student Affairs departments with assessment and evaluation projects to gather data on events, programs, and student learning for university accreditation and accolades. Many of these offices also create and promote in-house professional development opportunities for student affairs staff and encourage participation in regional and national professional development experiences.

Campus Ministries

Campus ministries is an umbrella term for the spirituality- and faith-based organizations and units within colleges and universities. This area of student affairs assists students with their spiritual and faith journey, as well as the practice of varying religions.

Career Services

Career services, or the career center, assists students through career exploration and skill acquisition in the job search and placement processes. They facilitate career assessments to help students determine potential paths, provide resources related to résumé writing and interview skills, and arrange interviews for internships and jobs with employers.

Development and Fund-Raising

The development and fund-raising office builds relationships with alumni, friends of the institution, and corporate entities and seeks contributions of time, talent, and (especially) treasure to better the overall campus community. People in development roles tend to work closely with the alumni affairs office and various other units within the Division of Student Affairs.

Fraternity and Sorority Affairs (or Greek Life)

Fraternity and sorority affairs offices serve as the clearinghouse for all social fraternities and sororities at the institution, including chapters from the National Panhellenic Council (NPC), Interfraternity Council (IFC), National Pan-Hellenic Conference (NPHC), National Association of Latino/Latina Fraternal Organizations (NALFO), and the Multicultural Greek Council (MGC or MCGC). They are the liaison between fraternity and sorority international headquarters, the local advisors and alumni, and the local chapters.

Health and Wellness (or Student Health and Campus Recreation)

Health and wellness, or student health and campus recreation, offices focus on the physical health and wellness of students. They provide a multitude of opportunities for aiding students when medical needs arise and providing recreational opportunities, including but not limited to working out, playing sports, and exploring outdoor adventures. These offices also encourage health and wellness through proactive health promotion campaigns such as nutrition and dietician services, smart choices with substances, and sexual health.

Human Resources

Human resources areas within Divisions of Student Affairs concentrate on the hiring, promotion, growth, and evaluation of staff. They aid staff in obtaining information about salary, benefits, and training and development opportunities.

Information Technology

Information technology units provide assistance to the Division of Student Affairs with both day-to-day computing needs and the creation and management of websites, web and data management systems, social media, and other similar tools.

Leadership and Service

Leadership and service offices aim to craft opportunities for students to serve and lead locally and globally. They tend to offer curricular or cocurricular courses in leadership, host leadership conferences and institutes, collaborate with nonprofit agencies to create hands-on service projects, and advise student groups on philanthropic endeavors.

Orientation or First-Year Experience

Orientation or first-year experience (or transitions) areas seek to create seamless transitions for students entering the institution. They offer a variety of programs and courses to acclimate students and their families to academic and social aspects of the institution and aid the process of institutional acculturation and socialization.

Residence Life or University Housing

Making campus home for students, in the literal sense, is the primary role of residence life or university housing. These offices manage facilities where students live and learn on a daily basis and create intentional programming to help students create and maintain healthy, balanced lives.

Student Activities and Student Unions

Student activities and the university unions provide facilities, programming, and involvement opportunities for students to engage socially, explore culture and arts, purchase books and merchandise, dine, handle mail, and utilize other auxiliary services. These facilities and programs are often viewed as the hub of campus life for students because they tend to serve as the location for student organization meetings and events, and they welcome visitors to campus daily.

Study Abroad

Study abroad offices guide students in their pursuit of academic studies outside the home institution, particularly study in other countries. They offer set programs where institutional faculty take students to another location and teach academic classes, and they help students who seek study at a different institution in another country locate resources. Study abroad programs range from a few weeks to an entire year.

Underrepresented Students (Multicultural Affairs, LGBTQ, Women's Center, Veterans' Affairs, "Nontraditional")

There are a variety of offices and centers that serve the needs of the campus's underrepresented populations, including but not limited to racial and ethnic minorities, women, veterans, "nontraditional" students, and LGBTQ students. The setup of these offices and centers varies; sometimes they are part of student affairs, and other times they are tied to a component of academic affairs. The purpose of these areas is to assist underrepresented populations in their access to, acclimation to, and success within the institution. They tend to be a "home away from home" for their populations and offer both awareness of and advocacy for the population, including but not limited to academic support, social programming, and calls for inclusion.

Chapter Summary

Understanding the ever-changing demographics of student populations and the multitude of roles student affairs can play in students' journey of learning and development is an essential aspect of comprehending the philosophy and purpose of the field of student affairs. After you grasp the philosophy and purpose, you are then faced with the conception of the logistics. It is important to know the various ways the Division of Student Affairs (or Student Life) can be structured, both in the larger institutional context and then within the divisional makeup for functional areas. Furthermore, it would benefit anyone interested in the field to research or, better yet, experience as many of the functional areas as possible to discern one's interest in working with those areas. These are the basic building blocks for examining the field of student affairs: students, roles, structure, and function.

Once you have decided the field is one in which you have interest, it may behoove you to hear more about what supervisors, new professionals, and national associations say are key skills and knowledge that lead to student affairs educators' success or downfall. The following chapter gives a brief literature review on these matters.

2

NEW PROFESSIONALS THROUGH THE MAGNIFYING MIRROR

When we want to see how we might appear to others, what do we tend to do? I, for one, often walk over to a shiny surface and take a look at my reflection. Mirrors provide an outside perspective that gives us a glance at parts of us we cannot always easily see. Even better than your typical, run-of-the-mill mirror is the simultaneously helpful and horrendous gadget called a magnifying mirror. You know what I am talking about . . . the mirror that you flip to its other side that makes your face 10 times as large and forces you to see your assets and shortcomings with glaring obviousness. That is the point of this chapter. To have a glance at new professionals—like you and, quite a few years ago, me—through the critical eye of a proverbial magnifying mirror. This mirror is the reflection of new professionals from the perspective of peers, supervisors, upper-level administrators, and researchers.

Will you always like what you see? No. Will you always agree? No. Is it a completely accurate assessment? Maybe not. However, it is useful to take a look and examine the good, the bad, and, possibly, the ugly that is often associated with new professionals like you and your peers.

Who Are You and Your Peers?

As you enter the field of higher education, or remain in it, you might be interested in knowing some information about the people who will become your peers. You may also want to gain insight on how others may perceive you.

New professionals are defined as first-time, full-time student affairs educators with experience ranging from 0 to 5 years and representing approximately 15% to 20% of people in the field (as cited in Renn & Hodges, 2007, p. 367). You and your peers will find the way to student affairs from a multitude of academic backgrounds at every type of college and university and will work in all types of settings, including but not limited to community colleges, four-year public and private institutions, for-profit institutions, and online institutions (Hirt, 2006). There is not necessarily a "typical" path into student affairs (you know this!); however, you, and many of your peers, will have a story about how you either treasured or abhorred your collegiate experience and, thus, want to assist current college students in having a positive academic and social experience during their time at the institution. Regardless of how you and your peers found a career in higher education, you will all embark upon your careers as student affairs educators with certain beliefs about how things should work.

What Are Your Ideal Expectations, and What Is the Reality?

There are many articles and books that discuss new professionals and what they expect from themselves, their supervisors, and their institutions. Collectively, I believe the following list aptly describes what you and your peers may be looking for as you enter the field of student affairs.

To Use Theory

You were told that you needed a graduate degree to be eligible for jobs in most student affairs divisions. In turn, you, reasonably, expect that your degree, and the theory that comes with it, matters. And, it does in a lot of ways. However, it can be a tough transition when you have been focused on learning theory and discussing how you see it in practice and then you begin to recognize that theory is not something that is at the forefront of daily work in student affairs. You may even find it frustrating when you bring up theory in meetings or with colleagues and get shut down verbally or nonverbally by others.

This may be unpopular to tell you, but this situation is a classic case of you valuing what you *know* and your employer valuing what you have *done*. Sure, you can spout theory all day, but can you advise, supervise, event plan, manage crises, and so on? Do you have the practical knowledge to match the theory? If so, kudos! If not, get to putting that theory to practice.

To Be Welcomed and Socialized

Many of your graduate programs have pontificated how you should expect that your office and institution will be prepared to welcome you to your new role through orientation and transition experiences. Effectively, you were told to expect to be socialized. Socialization is the process by which new members of an organization come to understand, appreciate, and adopt the customs, traditions, values, and goals of their profession and their new organization (Tull, Hirt, & Saunders, 2009). It is understandable why you expect this. You are, most likely, in a new environment or role, and you want to understand the philosophy and procedures of the institution, be introduced to the campus and student affairs culture, have outlined expectations for your job performance, and create and maintain connections to colleagues. And you want to have real, sit-down conversations about those things, not just learn about them through experiences of trial and error. You expect to have role models of socialization in your supervisor, colleagues, and divisional leaders. You want to discuss and witness how people follow procedure, make decisions, deal with politics, and manage time, among other things.

None of these are unfounded expectations. However, they may not always correspond with reality. Sometimes, you have to take socialization into your own hands. For more detailed information about the socialization process, please refer to Tull et al.'s (2009) book *Becoming Socialized in Student Affairs Administration: A Guide for New Professionals and Their Supervisors.*

To Be Utilized

You come to your institution with many skills and talents to offer, and you hope, and expect, that those skills and talents will be utilized. You want projects to call your own, desire autonomy to get the job done, and crave to be sought out for the expertise you believe you possess. In short, you want to feel like you matter and can make a difference. Who doesn't want that?

And sometimes it will happen. There will be days when your supervisor gives you a project and lets you run with it, knowing you are capable and will be successful. And sometimes it will not happen. You may not be invited to contribute to the aspect of your office that you care about most. Know that the balance will all work out over time.

To Be Included

Inclusion is a broad term that basically means that you feel like a part of a larger whole and that your part is valuable. As a new professional, you want to feel included, at the least, within your office and in the division. You want to be asked to help with projects handled by your office that are outside of your direct job, you seek opportunities to serve on committees, you aspire to teach classes, and you desire to be part of decision-making processes. You, probably more than any other population of student affairs educators, expect to contribute to the overall fabric of the institution.

For the most part, you will be included, just maybe not how you want to be included. Your supervisor and office will need you for "all hands on deck" situations. You will have opportunities to join committees, although you may not get your first choice ones. You may be asked to present workshops, facilitate trainings, and teach classes. You may even be asked for feedback during decision-making processes. But, inclusion will be a process that takes time. You will need time to show your knowledge and skills, and people will need time to realize and utilize them.

To Have a Voice and Be Heard

After being asked, or even cajoled, into sharing your thoughts and feelings in the classroom for a couple of years (or more), you will likely expect to have a voice in your new job—both literally and figuratively. You want colleagues and supervisors to ask for your opinion. You want to share your beliefs in meetings. You want to talk about what you learned in graduate school classes and from your experiences at other colleges and universities. You want to quote literature. Yet, you often find out, especially at large institutions, that hierarchy and politics can limit your sphere of influence.

Here's the deal: You can and do have a voice. You just have to be mindful about when and where you choose to use it in order for it to not only be heard but also be received. Speaking up about something with which you do not agree or proposing a new idea that is a bit radical is best saved for one-on-one meetings with supervisors and brainstorming with peers rather than blurted out in a department or division meeting or in front of upper-level administrators. It also helps to "do your homework." I know you thought that was over, but it never is. (See Chapter 4 on lifelong learning.) For your voice to be more heard and, hopefully, better received, you need to back up your personal support with research and facts from reputable sources and provide examples from similar peer institutions.

To Have a Good Supervisor

Your graduate program may have also entrenched in you that when you are job searching, a vital aspect of the search is finding good supervisors. You likely agreed with this. You probably seek to work with someone who has mastered the craft of supervision and understands what you expect and how to provide you with a primarily positive learning environment and workplace. You want your supervisor to guide you, support you, and challenge you (even if you do not recognize that you want your supervisor to do this). You are also probably looking for a supervisor who can serve as a mentor in the field.

There is a catch here: Many supervisors of new professionals like you are only a few years ahead of you in experience. They may or may not have any practice being in the supervisor role, because graduate schools do not tend to teach that skill. Supervision is mostly learned through actual supervising. So, much like you hope your supervisors leave you some room for learning and growth (i.e., error), you need to do the same for them. Another disconnect in this process is that your supervisor is not necessarily looking to be a mentor, which means that you may have to look elsewhere to have someone fill that role for you. That leads to the next expectation.

To Have Support Systems

In addition to having good supervisors, you typically expect to create and maintain support systems, including networks of both colleagues and mentors. You have often been informed that it is a smart idea to start this process with your graduate school cohorts, particularly as people move onward and upward in their career paths. You will be eager to develop similar cohorts as you begin your first jobs. You look for other new professionals to connect with on campus and often expect, or secretly hope, that your office or division will set up opportunities for networking and connecting through new professional groups, happy hours, or other social activities.

The reality is that creating these cohorts is often a task that you will have to take up on your own accord. Collect some e-mails or phone numbers and set up the lunch or happy hour session. Ask others to come together for a book or article of the month club. Set up an intramural sports or trivia team. The same goes for finding mentors. If your supervisor is not willing or able to serve as a mentor, you may find yourself at a loss for how to locate a mentor and develop that relationship. Although you might hope your colleagues or someone at the college or university will assist you with this endeavor, it is, yet again, something you will have to learn to do for yourself. When you meet people whose experiences, knowledge, and persona you value, ask them if they would be open to chatting with you. Build a relationship. Keep in contact. Cultivate a mentorship. (See Chapter 7 on networking and connecting.)

To Find and Maintain Balance or Integration

Finally, you expect and hope to have opportunities for balance or integration. (*Balance* and *integration* are both used here because people tend to prefer one term over the other.) I think that is a fair expectation; others may not agree with me because "you know about the crazy hours when you choose to go into a career in student affairs." However, you should never have to give up your life in order to work.

If no one has an intentional conversation with you about this topic, you may look to your colleagues and supervisors to determine how time and self-care are handled at the institution: Are people working crazy hours? Are they answering e-mail at 11:00 p.m. or 5:00 a.m.? Is there an option for comp or flex time? Do people use their vacation time? You will be transitioning out of a graduate school schedule and will often not know what do to with the time you had been spending in class or studying. Thus, you may naturally fill this time with more work hours than you probably should, which is the trap I fell into in my first and second jobs! You expect colleagues and supervisors to help you learn how to balance, or integrate, your time so that you can foster both a professional life and a personal life.

Some truth for you, folks: You have to figure out how to manage your time and create the balance or integration that you need. Regardless of how you want to spend your personal time (exercising, reading, dining out, watching TV, traveling, etc.), it is up to you to make that personal time end up on your calendar. You also have more ability to control your schedule than you might realize. Sure, you may have to work late a few days a week or a weekend every so often (more often for some than others). But, you can also sign up for yoga once a week or set up a play date for your pet or child. You can make dinner plans for every Thursday or plan a trip (or staycation) every 6 weeks. And, you can put those personal items in your calendar and treat them in equal regard to your work commitments. The choice is yours.

What Are the Career Themes You Might Want to Consider?

In addition to your expectations, Renn and Hodges (2007) discussed three career themes in their NASPA article titled "The First Year on the Job: Experiences of New Professionals in Student Affairs" that you might want to consider as you begin, and progress through, your career. You may want to focus on finding, or strengthening, these career elements:

- *Relationships* with supervisors, supervisees, students, mentors, colleagues, family, and friends
- *Fit* with the institution, with the job, and beyond the institution to the area in which it was located
- *Competence and confidence*, a continuum of knowledge and feeling that rests primarily on issues of job training, skills, and knowledge of one's role, strengths, and areas of improvement (Renn & Hodges, 2007)

Although Renn and Hodges used the themes to describe your first year, I think they also aptly apply throughout your career in higher education.

Relationships are relevant. Period. They matter professionally and personally, and they influence how we operate on a daily basis. Your career will be shaped by whom you know and by who knows you. It is vital to build a network of connections at your institution and around the region and, even, country. Building these relationships will create a support system for you and will allow you many outlets from which to gather information to do your job well. It is also important to take time to concentrate on your personal relationships with family, partners, friends, and so on. People tend to operate better professionally when their personal lives also get some attention. Let's also note that relationships are complex and time-consuming, regardless of context. It will be a task to create a relationship with your supervisor and with the students, just like it will be a task to maintain relationships with loved ones. So make sure to allocate appropriate amounts of time and effort to nurture all the relationships in your life.

Fit is fundamental. Feeling like your values and goals match that of your position and the institution is essential. Knowing you have both things to contribute and things to learn in your role is important. Finding ways to personally connect in the area where you live is critical. These will carry across every job you have, no matter how many times you switch roles or move locations. You will want to feel like it fits, like you fit. It is also notable that sometimes the job may fit better than the location or vice versa. Sacrifices are made sometimes to get out of one situation or into another. You just have to decide what aspect of fit is most valuable to you at that point: professional fit or personal fit. And jump for joy when the two align (at least for the most part)!

Feeling confident and competent is crucial. The first step is knowing what is expected of you in the role: What are your responsibilities, and what are the priorities for the position or office? You have knowledge and talents to give to your role and the institution, and you want those things to be utilized and further developed. You should also want to learn more, to gain from your new role and experiences. It is important to express both of those—what you have to give and to gain—to your supervisors and supervisees. It is also necessary to assess what areas are strengths for you and what areas can be improved. This helps feed feelings of confidence and competence because you are aware of what you are good at and how you need help from others to get the job done well. Confidence and competence tend to operate on a continuum, though. Some days you may feel like a rock star on one end of the spectrum, and other days you may feel like a buffoon on the other end. It happens. What you are looking for is what is known in sports as the "500 mark"—if you are feeling confidence and competence on more days than you are not, or a bit more than 50% of the time, you are doing well!

These three themes—relationships, fit, and confidence and competence—will follow you throughout your career as a student affairs educator, no matter your functional area or institutional type. So it would behoove you to give time and attention to how you build and nurture relationships and networks, find and cultivate fit, and construct confidence and competence.

Which Skills Do You Have, and Which Ones Are Useful?

(Please note: These are not one and the same.) Part of the confidence and competence theme discussed in the previous section depends on your ability to attain and sustain skill sets. Although there are countless skills that could be useful for you, studies by Waple (2006) and Cuyjet, Longwell-Grice, and Molina (2009) pinpointed what seem to be the most vital skills for people in the field of student affairs. These skills include student development theory, oral and written communication skills, ethics and standards of practice, multicultural awareness and knowledge, working with diverse populations, career development, the history of student affairs, student demographics and characteristics, the history of higher education, problem solving, effective program planning and implementation, cultural foundations of higher education, legal issues in higher education, presentation skills, leadership theory, research methods, crisis and conflict management, organizational theory, advising students and student organizations, student outcomes assessment, program evaluation, supervision of staff, management theory, use of technology, campus and community relations, strategic planning, budget and fiscal management, grant writing, and writing for publication (Cuyjet et al., 2009; Waple, 2006, p. 9). Out of this somewhat exhaustive list, there are skills that you attained at higher levels than others during the graduate school experience in higher education and student affairs programs.

High-Status Attainment

Waple's (2006) study explored how your peers rated their skill attainment from their graduate programs and how useful they found those skills to be in their first job. The findings of the study point out that your peers often arrived to their first jobs with strong understandings of the following 10 skills:

1. Student development theory
2. Oral and written communication skills
3. Ethics in student affairs work
4. Multicultural awareness and knowledge
5. Career development

6. History of student affairs
7. Student demographics and characteristics
8. History of higher education
9. Problem solving
10. Effective program planning and implementation (Waple, 2006, p. 9)

Although it is always beneficial to have skills, the concern with this list is that some of the skills that your peers attained at a high status were not found to be very useful in their first jobs, especially the history of student affairs and the history of higher education.

Cuyjet et al.'s (2009) study investigated the perceptions of skill attainment from your peers and their supervisors and compared the perceptions to identify if your peers and their supervisors had congruent impressions about skill attainment. Similar to Waple's earlier study, Cuyjet et al.'s study examined not only the level with which skills were attained but also the practicality of those skills. Cuyjet et al.'s study found that your peers believed they attained student development and ethics and standards at a high level, which aligns with Waple's earlier study. In addition, comparable to findings in Waple's study, your peers in this study felt the most important skills they learned were ethics and standards, working with diverse populations, and student development theory. Supervisors of your peers had similar perceptions. They found your peers to be well versed in student development theory and working with diverse populations, which they believed to be beneficial in student affairs work, along with ethics.

Low-Status Attainment

Graduate preparation programs cannot teach everything, and you and your supervisors and institutions should not expect that to be the case. Waple's (2006) study highlighted a few areas to which graduate programs do not pay much time or attention. Your peers noted that they did not feel they received much instruction in the following areas:

- Use of technology
- Budget and fiscal management
- Strategic planning
- Campus and community relations (i.e., politics)
- Supervision
- Assessment (Waple, 2006, p. 9)

The issue is that some of these skills in the low-status category also happen to be some of the same skills that your peers stated were necessary in their first jobs, particularly the use of technology and supervision (Waple, 2006). Cuyjet et al.'s (2009) study found similar concerns. Your peers listed grant writing, budget and fiscal management, and supervision as skills they were lacking after graduate school, and their supervisors agreed with them.

Low-status attainment in budget and fiscal management, grant writing, and supervision may not seem like a significant issue in your first job; however, some of your peers are tasked with the supervision of graduate students or student workers and with managing program budgets. Knowing your peers did not gain much experience in graduate school in these areas, supervisors and departments must provide assistance to you and your peers in these areas or direct you to training or other professional development options in order to aid you in being successful in these aspects of your role.

In What Areas Should You Focus Your Professional Development?

Regardless of the level of skill attainment you and your peers received from your graduate preparation programs, you will need continuous opportunities for learning in order to further develop as student affairs educators. (See Chapter 4 on lifelong learning.) One way to grow and learn is through professional development. (See Chapter 6 on professional development.) ACPA conducted a study in 2007 to determine what were your and your peers' top professional development needs. You and your peers ranked the following six needs as your most important areas of professional development:

1. Receiving adequate support
2. Understanding job expectations
3. Fostering student learning
4. Moving up in the field of student affairs
5. Enhancing supervision skills
6. Developing multicultural competence

It makes sense that at least three of your six needs correspond with skills from Waple's and Cuyjet et al.'s studies. You know that there is always more to learn in areas like student learning and multicultural competence, and you recognize that you will need to gain in areas like supervision skills and fiscal management in order to advance in the field. Chapter 6 of this book will focus more intently on professional development.

In What Areas Should You Strive to Be Competent?

In 2010, the NASPA and ACPA organizations collaborated to define the top 10 professional competencies, including "knowledge, skills, and attitudes" expected of student affairs educators (ACPA and NASPA Joint Task Force on Professional Competencies, 2010, p. 3). These competencies serve as a benchmark not only for professional development experiences created by the national organizations but also for your own personal assessment. Each competency and its overall definition as outlined by NASPA and ACPA is listed in this section. It would be a good idea to conduct a self-assessment on if, and how, you meet and feel confident in these competency areas. For more information on the basic, intermediate, and advanced levels of each competency, please visit the NASPA website (www.naspa.org/programs/profdev) or the ACPA website (www2.myacpa.org/professional-development/resources).

Advising and Helping

The Advising and Helping competency area addresses the knowledge, skills, and attitudes related to providing counseling and advising, support, direction, feedback, critique, referrals, and guidance to individuals and groups.

Assessment, Evaluation, and Research

The Assessment, Evaluation, and Research competency area focuses on the ability to use, design, conduct, and critique qualitative and quantitative assessment, evaluation, and research analyses; to manage organizations using assessment, evaluation, and research processes and the results obtained from them; and to shape the political and ethical climate surrounding assessment, evaluation, and research processes and uses on campus.

Equity, Diversity, and Inclusion

The Equity, Diversity, and Inclusion competency area includes the knowledge, skills, and attitudes needed to create learning environments that are enriched with diverse views and people. It is also designed to create an institutional ethos that accepts and celebrates differences among people, helping to free them of any misconceptions and prejudices.

Ethical Professional Practice

The Ethical Professional Practice competency area pertains to the knowledge, skills, and attitudes needed to understand and apply ethical standards to one's work. Although ethics is an integral component of all the competency areas, this competency area focuses specifically on the integration of ethics into all aspects of self and professional practice.

History, Philosophy, and Values

The History, Philosophy, and Values competency area involves knowledge, skills, and attitudes that connect the history, philosophy, and values of the profession to one's current professional practice. This competency area embodies the foundations of the profession from which current and future research and practice will grow. The commitment to demonstrating this competency area ensures that our present and future practices are informed by an understanding of our history, philosophy, and values.

Human and Organizational Resources

The Human and Organizational Resources competency area includes knowledge, skills, and attitudes used in the selection, supervision, motivation, and formal evaluation of staff; conflict resolution; management of the politics of organizational discourse; and the effective application of strategies and techniques associated with financial resources, facilities management, fundraising, technology use, crisis management, risk management, and sustainable resources.

Law, Policy, and Governance

The Law, Policy, and Governance competency area includes the knowledge, skills, and attitudes relating to policy development processes used in various contexts, the application of legal constructs, and the understanding of governance structures and their effect on one's professional practice.

Leadership

The Leadership competency area addresses the knowledge, skills, and attitudes required of a leader, whether it be a positional leader or a member of the staff, both in an individual capacity and within a process of how individuals work together effectively to envision, plan, and effect change in organizations and respond to internal and external constituencies and issues.

Personal Foundations

The Personal Foundations competency area involves the knowledge, skills, and attitudes to maintain emotional, physical, social, environmental, relational, spiritual, and intellectual wellness; be self-directed and self-reflective; maintain excellence and integrity in work; be comfortable with ambiguity;

be aware of one's own areas of strength and growth; have a passion for work; and remain curious.

Student Learning and Development

The Student Learning and Development competency area addresses the concepts and principles of student development and learning theory. This includes the ability to apply theory to improve and inform student affairs practice, as well as to understand teaching and training theory and practice.

Chapter Summary

Let's review what our glance in the magnifying mirror has shown us. You and your peers are new professionals—individuals who are still in the beginning stages of your career as student affairs educators. You arrive at colleges and universities with a host of expectations, knowledge, and skills, and you recognize that you are charged with possessing, or learning, multiple competencies in order to be successful in the field.

I believe it is the role of all of us in higher education to welcome you and help you become socialized in student affairs, which includes helping you navigate themes we see in our own careers—such as relationships, fit, and confidence and competence—and challenging you to take ownership and create your own career strategies.

3

CREATING A STUDENT AFFAIRS CAREER STRATEGY

Strategy:

- a careful plan or method: a clever stratagem
- the art of devising or employing plans or stratagems toward a goal
- an adaptation or complex of adaptations (as of behavior, metabolism, or structure) that serves or appears to serve an important function in achieving evolutionary success (Strategy, n.d.)

*I*ntentionality. *Strategy. Plan.* Those are three words that are thrown around a lot in the field of higher education. We create mission and vision statements. We establish values. We discuss goals and objectives and how we plan to determine if, when, and how we have met them. We craft branding and marketing campaigns to inform others of our offerings. On a yearly basis, or more, we are asked to reflect on and strategize for our jobs. But how often do we do that for ourselves? How often do we give ample time and attention to establishing a career strategy? Not often enough, I would argue, and not with the same intentionality that we strategize for our offices. It is time to change that. It is time to give our own career strategy the same scrutiny and care that we give to our job.

Intentional and Spontaneous

There are two methods to crafting your career strategy: being intentional and leaving room for the spontaneous to occur. Both are important to your strategy. That may sound odd, but it is the truth. Let me explain.

Intentionality means you make time and dedicate effort to reflect on and construct a strategy for yourself. It means that you assess what skills and experiences you possess and what skills and experiences you need to gain. Intentionality means that you reflect on and determine how you can go about demonstrating what skills and experiences you have and how you can go about gaining what you need. It means setting goals for when you want to accomplish it all, determining who can help you along the path, and understanding why you are doing all of it. Intentionality means you have purpose. It also suggests that you can answer that ever-appearing interview question, "Where do you see yourself in 1, 5, and 10 years?" I do not like that question; I never have. I think it asks us to predict something that we cannot. However, I understand why it is asked. People are trying to determine if you can plan, strategize, reflect, and project. Do you have a purpose and goals? Do you care as much about your own development as you do the development of others? How can you plan to assist students or staff in their growth if you never pay attention to your own?

But, as anyone in higher education knows, plans do not typically work out as they are written or discussed. Rather, plans are a framework for direction that ebb and flow based on environmental circumstances. It is why we have backup plans, risk management plans, and crisis management plans. We know plans go awry. And that is all right. It is the process of planning that matters more than the exact plan coming to fruition. What we should be reaching for is not perfection but, rather, progress. As long as we are making gains in the direction of our goals and visions, we are doing it right. Plus, we ought to leave room for unexpected opportunities for learning, because those are sometimes the best lessons.

Leaving room for the spontaneous speaks to the parts of your career plan that you did not know existed or that you did not specifically seek out. These are the opportunities that happen to you. Things you are "voluntold" to do. Spontaneous opportunities may be committees you are required, or asked, to sit on. They may be presentations someone seeks you out to facilitate. These chances are the random professional development webinars, connections, and conversations that fall into your lap. It may even be the job posting someone forwards to you just to say, "Hey, thought of you when I saw this!" All of these spontaneous instances can derail—mostly in a good way!—our purposeful plans, our tactical strategies. But, we must leave room for them. These are the opportunities that help open our minds to prospects that may not have been on our radar and that can initiate new directions and strategies.

Therefore, it is a "both–and" concept rather than a traditional either–or concept. We should be *both* intentional in our career strategy *and* willing to embrace the spontaneous. It is only when we achieve this "both–and" that we will be able to fully discover the possibilities that lie within our career path.

Strategy Is Not a Straitjacket

Here is the thing about a plan or checklist or strategy: We often lock ourselves into it. We do not want to deviate from the plan. We want to be able to check off all the items on the list. We want to be able to say that our strategy worked like it was projected. And, we know that in reality that is extremely unlikely to occur. Some of our plans will come to fruition. We will check the majority of the items off the list. The strategy will mostly work. Here's the truth: Strategy is not a straitjacket. It is not intended to be. We do not want to lock ourselves so firmly into a strategy that we leave no room for movement, adaptability, or growth.

Let's continue with the jacket analogy. Rather than a straitjacket, strategy is like your favorite blazer: appropriate for most occasions because you can dress it up or dress it down to fit the environment, well suited (no pun intended) for you because it has been fit to your needs, and enduring if you choose a classic cut and color. It allows for both flexibility and sustainability. Eventually, though, that blazer, like your career strategy, will need to be updated. Think again of that 1-, 5-, and 10-year question. Your initial career strategy may work for the first 10 years of your career if you do it well, then it will be time to craft a new career strategy for the next phase of your career.

Reflecting on Your Current Strategy (or Lack Thereof)

Now that we know what a career strategy is and is not, it is crucial for us to stop and conduct some self-assessment and engage in reflection on our current career strategy, or lack thereof. We cannot know where we are going if we do not know where we have been or where we currently are. Please take time to deeply consider the following questions (see also Appendix A):

- What are my career goals for 1, 3, 5, 10 years from now? What is my ultimate career goal? (Or, to whose job on campus do I aspire, and why? How would I go about making myself qualified for that job?)
- What kinds of educational credentials (formal and informal) do I have? Will my current education level get me to my career goal or ideal job?
- What experiences and skill sets, both job related and volunteer, do I currently have on my résumé? Are there experiences and skills that I think I need in addition to those?
- Do I have a professional development plan? Do I know how to create one?
- Am I comfortable with networking or connecting? Why or why not? What strategies do I normally use in networking or connecting?

- Do I frequently take time to reflect on my career? Do I assess where I am and where I would like to be and adjust my time and experiences to reflect my goals? What strategies can I use to reflect?

After completing the self-reflection, you should have an idea about where your career has given you ample opportunities for growth and development and where you would like to continue, or begin, further learning. You should also, hopefully, feel called to revisit these questions on a yearly basis, or more, just like you do for your job. Each time you pull out your office's strategic planning documents, also pull out this self-reflection worksheet or a similar document. Your career strategy needs the same attention you give to your office's strategy! Much like your institution's assessment administrator may provide you with guidelines in developing your office's strategic plan, the following five career strategy components can act as standards in your efforts to craft your personal career strategy and establish a fulfilling career.

Five Career Strategy Components

Career strategies can be broken down into five different yet intertwined components or tactics. Some would argue that there is much overlap between the tactics, and they are right. However, there is enough distinction between each tactic to think about them independently first and then see how they weave together to create a holistic career strategy and path. The five career strategy components are (a) lifelong learning, (b) extending your experiences, (c) planning for professional development, (d) networking or connecting, and (e) self-reflection. Each component is a vital tactic to your career strategy and should be addressed in your career plan.

Lifelong Learning

As educators, we espouse a belief in lifelong learning. But, do we live it? *Lifelong learning* is defined as both formal and informal learning experiences or educational opportunities. The formal aspect of lifelong learning includes but is not limited to master's and doctoral programs in education, counseling, social work, and public administration, among others. The informal opportunities for lifelong learning can consist of taking self-development and betterment courses, volunteering, shadowing, interning, attending conferences and institutes, conducting committee work, reading literature and research, and engaging in intentional conversations with colleagues and students. Lifelong learning will be discussed in Chapter 4.

Extending Your Experiences

We often work with our students to assist them in deciphering what they are gaining through their experiences on campus through involvement and in whatever workplace they may be employed. Do we do this for ourselves too? Do we take time to decode our job descriptions or to discern the transferable skills that we possess through our experiences? Extending your experiences is about understanding not only what you are gaining through your formal employment but also how doing committee work, volunteering at all levels, and having personal interests outside of your "day job" can take your experiences to another level and impact your career. Extending your experiences will be considered in Chapter 5.

Planning for Professional Development

Have your supervisors ever asked you to complete a "PD plan"? If not, shame on them! If so, did you take it seriously? You should have. Your professional development is key to keeping your mind and your career fresh and to constructing your career strategy. Closely tied to the concepts of lifelong learning and extending your experiences, professional development is about putting your career plan on paper and deciding when, where, and how you will continue to develop and with whom you hope to interact and learn. Now, I know you may be thinking, "PD takes money, and neither my institution nor I have any to spare." Although professional development can be costly in some respects, it is important to get creative and think outside of the norm when planning for your professional development. Methods of resourceful and innovative professional development will be examined in Chapter 6.

Networking or Connecting

How many times have you heard someone say, "This is such a small field"? My guess is frequently. However, not everyone feels this way, particularly if they are just entering the student affairs world or making the transition from another aspect of higher education or nonprofit management. It is essential that you think about the methods you want to employ to seek out others—peers, mentors, and faculty colleagues—in higher education to build relationships and assist you along your career path. We use both the terms *networking* and *connecting* because we know that people react differently to these kinds of terms. People tend to think of networking as something for the extroverted that occurs in large spaces with a seemingly excessive amount of individuals. This perception can be overwhelming; thus, we simultaneously use the term *connecting*, which we define as getting to know others through commonalities.

We encourage you to use whichever term and method feel authentic to you, in both philosophy and format. We also want to mention that politics can come into play with this tactic. Politics are real at higher education institutions, whether public or private, within the larger field, and with external constituents. Approaches to networking or connecting and navigating politics will be offered in Chapter 7.

Self-Reflection

If you have ever created and implemented an assessment for one of your office's programs or events, you have likely asked students to partake in some self-reflection. Do you practice that yourself as well? If so, kudos! If not, I challenge you to do so. And, it is up to you to determine how to reflect. Some examples of how we know student affairs educators engage in reflection will be offered; however, what works for me may not work for you and vice versa. I encourage you to "do you" when it comes to reflection. Try various techniques and determine what works for you. Then recognize that practice makes productive—the more you engage in self-reflection, the more productive that process will become for you. Reflection on self-reflection will occur in Chapter 8.

Chapter Summary

Intentionality. Strategy. Plan. Take some time to implement these concepts for your career, not in a way that is stifling or rigid but in a way that allows you to thrive over the long term. Know that purposeful decision making is key and that sometimes the spontaneous will occur, and you will incorporate it in the best way you know how. Ask key questions regularly to help you reflect on your career and the strategy you use to shape it. Then, use the five components—lifelong learning, extending your experiences, planning for professional development, networking or connecting, and self-reflection—that are introduced here, and further explained in subsequent chapters, to explore and establish a growth and development framework that will aid you in your career aspirations.

4

LIFELONG LEARNING

With contributions by Mat Erpelding, Amber Garrison Duncan,
Sandra Miles, Laura Osteen, and Jeremiah Shinn

> *You should always be learning. If you are the smartest person in the room,*
> *you're in the wrong place.*
>
> —Erica Bearman

> *Anyone who stops learning is old, whether at twenty or eighty.*
> *Anyone who keeps learning stays young.*
>
> —Henry Ford

It is a firm belief of mine that if you intend to serve as an educator that you are also committed to the practice of the field—as a learner. Educators cannot encourage and challenge colleagues and students to learn unless they are engaging in the learning as well. Learning in higher education takes place in a variety of contexts, including but certainly not limited to formal degree programs at master's and doctoral levels and informal avenues of volunteering, shadowing, interning, attending conferences and institutes, serving on committees, reading literature, and having intentional conversations with colleagues and students. Furthermore, it is important to recognize that learning can occur anywhere and all the time if you pay attention, ask questions, actively listen, and appreciate others' perspectives and experiences.

Formal Processes of Learning

To pursue a career as a student affairs educator, you will be expected to engage in some formal learning and obtain a degree (or three). Most higher education administrator roles require a bachelor's degree; many institutions prefer, or require, a master's degree for entry-level positions; and as you climb the proverbial career ladder, you will even find positions that are doctorate preferred or required, sometimes for director roles and particularly for senior student affairs officer (SSAO) roles. We are a field full of advanced degrees, even if salaries do not necessarily reflect it!

After you make the decision that higher education is your field of choice, you should move on to the research and choice process for your formal schooling. Note that just because this will be the second (or third) go-around of college choice does not mean it will be easier. Picking the right fit may be even more important for graduate school than for your undergraduate experience. Why? Because your classes are much smaller and more discussion based. Because your faculty can make or break your degree process. Because you want solid work experience to leverage in the job market. Because you may want to teach, research, write, or publish.

Although rankings may be good public relations for programs, what you really want to know is if you can thrive in that program and at that institution. Saying you went to the [insert number] program in the country will not matter if your thesis or dissertation was not approved or if you have less than substantial hands-on experience in a Division of Student Affairs. So, let's talk about how to make some decisions when researching options for graduate school.

Degree Decisions

There are many considerations when discerning how to obtain a graduate degree that enables your eligibility for roles in student affairs. Putting degree program type (higher education, student affairs, counseling, social work, etc.) and requirements aside, let's focus on logistical choices of graduate school.

In Person Versus Online
Similar to many of today's life choices, when it comes to graduate school, you now have the option of pursing degrees in person, online, or through a hybrid format of both. Choosing which works best for your needs is a product of a self-assessment of your mobility, your own learning style, and your "on the ground" experiences in higher education.

Mobility is one of the first factors in considering graduate school format. You need to decide if you want to remain in your current location, if you have the ability to travel periodically, or if you have the latitude to permanently move (at least until program completion). If you are place bound, then you can research in-person programs in your immediate area or in close proximity or completely online programs. If episodic travel is an option, you can also check into hybrid programs that teach much of the content online while also requiring you to travel to the institution, or a nearby city, for in-person meetings for a number of weekends per semester or a couple of weeks during the summer. If you can relocate, you, obviously, have the most options available to you and should investigate all of the programs that interest you.

Once you filter your choices based on mobility, learning style becomes key when determining if an in-person, online, or hybrid format will work best for you. In-person programs typically give you more face time with faculty and other students on a weekly basis because you will see them during course instruction and have the option to visit faculty during office hours or set up in-person meetings with peers for group projects or study groups. They also tend to work best for auditory and kinesthetic learners. Hybrid formats provide some of the same direct benefits for the same types of learners, although in shorter stints than in-person programs. You would get some concentrated face-to-face time with your faculty and peers during weekend meetings or summer institutes that would allow you to put faces with the names and voices you interact with in your online courses. You can also get a feel for the institution if you are on campus during those meetings, which may aid the needs of kinesthetic learners. Online-only programs are probably best suited for visual learners who prefer indirect contact. Depending on how courses are set up, online programs may offer synchronous, asynchronous, or combination options. In synchronous courses all students sign in at a specific day and time, and the instructor conducts a live lesson that may include the ability of students to participate through either talk or text. Asynchronous courses allow students to access lessons at their convenience and focus on indirect participation methods through posting boards or e-mail conversations.

Regardless of people's learning style, degree program options that are fully online or hybrid would be best suited for people already working in higher education roles because principally online programs would not afford opportunities for assistantships, where many students gain their practical experiences. In-person programs, on the other hand, often require students to obtain graduate assistantships at the institution, or a nearby one, and participate in internships and/or practica with other functional areas or institutions in order to explore theory to practice initiatives and gain "on the ground" experiences to leverage during the job search.

Program format decisions should weigh heavily on mobility, learning style, and experience level. I cannot tell you which of those three is most important to you or your future employer, but I can tell you that those elements will shape which format best suits your needs for formal schooling.

Part-Time Versus Full-Time
Another aspect of degree decisions is making the call to attend the program in a part-time or full-time capacity. Part-time enrollment in graduate school

means you take one or two classes, which generally equates to 1 to 8 credit hours. Full-time enrollment typically means you have at least three classes, or 9 or more credit hours. This part of the graduate school decision often comes down to your financial and family situation and if you need, or want, to work full-time or can afford to scale back to part-time work. It is common that people who attend classes part-time often work full-time and vice versa. Many part-time students are working at the program institution or another one in the area while they work toward their degree; full-time students, on the other hand, often obtain graduate assistantships that allow them to work at the institution or a nearby one in a part-time role. However, I will note that there are some amazing people out there who have the capacity to both attend school full-time and work full-time while also tending to their personal lives. I tip my hat to these folks, because I am not confident that I could have been one of them.

The other element impacted by your enrollment status is the time to degree (i.e., when you will finish). It makes mathematical sense that people who have the ability to make more classes, or hours, each term will be able to complete the program more swiftly. Let's look at a program with 57 total credit hours, including both 45 course-work hours and 12 thesis or dissertation hours. If Person A is attending full-time in a semester-based program and enrolls in 9 hours per semester, he or she can complete course work in five semesters (not including any summer school). Person B, on the other hand, is attending part-time in the same semester-based program and enrolls in 6 hours per semester; it will take Person B seven to eight semesters (not including any summer school) to finish up course work.

This scenario may also carry over to the dissertation phase of a doctoral program or thesis stage of a master's program, although that is not always the case. People who attend full-time (theoretically) should have more time to write and, thus, finish the dissertation or thesis phase more quickly. It is important to note, though, that individuals' dissertation or thesis phase is unique based on their research topic, population, and methodology and how that may impact the Institutional Review Board (IRB) process, the data collection phase, and the response time of their chair and/or committee.

In short, there is no silver bullet to completing a program quickly, but people who have the option, and privilege, to attend full-time often have less time to degree (and probably more loan debt).

Straight Through Versus Time Off
A question often asked about formal schooling is, "When is a good time to go back to [graduate] school?" The answer to that is "never." It is never a "good" time to go back to school. There is always life stuff that needs attention.

There is usually not a time when you have a random pot of money sitting around for tuition and fees. So, do not wait for a good time.

The other time consideration is whether people should gain work experience before pursuing a graduate degree. The answer to this question is, "it depends." I would say that experience never hurts, and often it gives you perspective that better enables you to understand how to put course theory into practice. It is typical in higher education for undergraduate students to roll right into higher education or student affairs master's programs. Doctoral programs are a bit different. Many people are encouraged to, and do, take chunks of time between obtaining a master's degree and a doctoral degree. This reason for this is many jobs that require or prefer doctoral degrees also require, or prefer, a significant amount of years of experience (5–10 years) along with the doctorate. So, if you go straight through all of your formal schooling and end up with a doctorate and very little, if any, full-time work experience, you may face a situation of being overeducated for entry- or mid-level positions and underexperienced for higher-level positions that typically seek people who hold doctorates.

A final time consideration is the transition back to formal schooling after taking several, or many, years off. It can take some time to get back into the "school mode," especially if the technology used in schooling today is different from when you were an undergraduate (which is often the case). The transition back to reading, writing, attending class, and studying can sometimes be a rough one. The more time you take off between degrees, the more apprehension you may experience about reinstating your identity and practice as a student. Just think of graduate school and being a student in the bike-riding analogy—a skill once learned is never forgotten and will come back to you with time and practice.

Finding Fit

Out of all the aspects to decisions on graduate school degrees, I think this one is the core and incorporates all the others. You must find a program—master's or doctoral—that is a good fit for you professionally and personally. Does the program course work appeal you? Are the faculty members studying research topics that are aligned with your interests? Is the atmosphere collaborative or competitive, and which do you prefer? What is the Division of Student Affairs like there? What are the financial packages? Can you live in that town, city, state, or region? Are there social outlets for you?

Now, do not get it twisted. No program is perfect. The goal is to find one that is excellent for you. The key part there is—*for you*! It needs to meet your needs and desires. It needs to challenge you and support you. It needs to suit your learning style and appreciate your contributions. Rankings, faculty accolades, athletic teams, and other elements like those will not matter if you do not feel a fit with the program. So pay attention to your gut! And visit. I often find that when I walk onto a college campus (or take a virtual tour) and talk to a few folks, I know pretty quickly if it could be a fit for me or not.

Degree Designations

Once you decide to obtain formal schooling and have found some programs that fit your needs and wants, you then have to make the additional decision of which type of degree to pursue. There are at least three types of master's degrees and two types of doctoral degrees that align with work in higher education.

Master's Programs

You have three options of degree designation when pursuing a master's degree. Those include a master of arts (MA), a master of education (MEd), and a master of science (MS). The institution typically chooses which degree designation it will use for its program, and it may tie back into the overall Carnegie classification of the institution. For example, research-focused institutions will likely have MS programs, whereas master's colleges and universities will often offer MA or MEd programs (do a web search for "Carnegie classifications" to learn more).

Fields of study—majors or specializations—for master's degrees that typically lead to a career in student affairs can include but are not limited to the following: higher education, student affairs, college student personnel, counseling, social work, business administration, public administration, and nonprofit administration. Your choice of major may vary based on your personal interests or how you see the degree being used over time. The most direct choices for someone interested in student affairs would be a master's in higher education, student affairs, or college student personnel.

Does it matter? For the most part, employers will not care about your master's degree designation. Theoretically, an MS means your program was more science or research based, but employers are not really concerned with that. As long as you obtain a master's degree, you are qualified for all entry-level jobs in student affairs.

The same is true regarding field of study. Most entry-level and mid-level job postings read something like this for educational requirements: "MS/MA in student affairs, counseling in higher education, college student personnel, nonprofit administration, or related field." So, you have some options when it comes to choices of major.

Doctoral Programs

You have two options of degree designation when pursuing a doctoral degree. Those include a doctor of education (EdD) and a doctor of philosophy (PhD). The institution typically chooses which degree designation it will use for its program, and, again, it may tie back into the overall Carnegie classification of the institution. Another factor here is the amount of research classes, or credit hours, the program requires. EdD programs usually have lower requirements in research methodology courses, whereas PhD programs require at least five classes, or 15 credit hours, including two classes in the methodology (quantitative or qualitative) you are not planning to use for your dissertation and three to four classes in your chosen methodology.

Does it matter? Although I wish I could answer "no" here, and it sort of exasperates me that I cannot, the fact is that it often does matter in academia which type of doctoral degree you possess. True, sad story: Because education is the only field that offers EdD programs, scholars in other fields sometimes view it as the "easy" doctorate, even if that is a misguided assumption. The advice often given to people who are deciding between EdD programs and PhD programs is that the EdD is for people who plan to serve as administrators, whereas the PhD is for people who plan to serve as faculty or researchers. I would argue that administrators also benefit from a PhD if their work tends to involve collaboration with faculty, because faculty from other fields usually possess a PhD themselves and often hold more respect (whether or not they should) for colleagues who share their degree designation.

The unsettling part of this debate for me is that the difference between many EdD and PhD programs is that PhD programs often require their students to take one to three classes, or 3 to 9 credit hours, more in research methodology. That is it. Often, EdD students participate in some kind of comprehensive exam or project at the end of course work just like PhD students do and write dissertations with the same parameters that PhD students have. All this hoopla is over a couple of classes . . . and a lot of higher education history, pomp, and circumstance. And, at the end of the day, regardless of which kind of doctorate you obtain, you are still among the rare 1% of the U.S. population who possesses such a degree, and you can still have them call you "Doctor [insert name]" if you want.

Informal Processes of Learning

Educators know that learning does not, and should not, occur only through formal schooling processes. Student affairs educators, more specifically, have data—both empirical and anecdotal—that prove that just as much growth and development occur outside of the classroom as inside it. So, it would make sense to practice what is preached. And that is good news, because it means that (a) a lot of learning can be done at little to no cost and (b) learning can, and should, continue after all the formal schooling is completed. Although this section will not provide an exhaustive list of the informal processes of learning, it will give you some ideas of how to incorporate informal learning into your professional life.

Volunteering

This is a simple concept and is what it sounds like: the giving of your time and talent for free to a person, organization, department, or institution in exchange for experience. You can volunteer on the campus where you have a job, for another campus nearby, or for a local, state, regional, or national organization. You can volunteer in a professional capacity or a personal one. Offer to help with a campus event outside of your area: help residence life with move in, assist fraternity and sorority life with recruitment, or go out to recruit students with admissions. Join a local or regional civic organization to plan events for people in your area or commit to serve the less fortunate on a continual basis. As long as you are practicing current skills or acquiring new ones, the volunteer opportunity is worthwhile and will add to the repertoire of experiences on your résumé.

Interning

Interning is basically one step up from volunteering (and could possibly include a small stipend). Internships are often longer commitments than volunteer opportunities but still include sharing your time and talents with a person or organization outside of your usual daily position or office. They allow you to explore areas of interest and gain new proficiencies without changing, or fully committing, to a new job or organization.

Shadowing

Shadowing is another term you have probably heard before, and it means what it sounds like it does. Shadowing is asking to join someone for a day, week, or more to learn about what it is like to have his or her role (on campus or in the community). You would attend meetings with him or her, discuss responsibilities, talk about successes and struggles, and generally learn what it is like to operate in that capacity. This is a great option if you are trying to decide what your long-term career goals might be and want to get a better picture of what a specific role or position entails. The key to shadowing is to observe more than one person in the role so you can get a well-rounded viewpoint of what the role is like rather than what the role is like for that specific person. For example, if you wonder what it might be like to serve as a residence life director, inquire with several residence life directors in your area (or close proximity) about shadowing them for a day or two and then having some one-on-one meetings to discuss your observations over a semester-long period. You might be surprised at how willing people are to share their experiences. You would also, hopefully, walk away with a better understanding of a role, a functional area, and whether either of those is a fit for you.

Serving on Committees

Have you ever seen that bullet point "other duties as assigned" on your job description? Well, that responsibility often includes volunteering, or being "voluntold," for committee work on your campus. Serving as a member of the marketing committee, social justice committee, ethics committee, accreditation committee, awards committee, and countless others can be a part of your job or experiences to which you offer contributions. Although committee work often adds meetings to your schedule and lines on your to-do list, committees are valuable learning opportunities that provide experiences that directly and indirectly relate to your job and grow your skill sets. Outside of the college or university, there are also openings for committee memberships with local, state, regional, and national organizations, including higher education associations and associations of personal interest to you. Think of committee work as a chance to practice skills that you may not get to use in your daily work, and volunteer for committee tasks that allow you to acquire or strengthen skills that could propel your career forward.

Reading Literature

Not all people find joy in reading like I do. However, keeping abreast of both the foundational literature and the recent literature in higher education is important to exercising your mind and providing you with benchmarks and new ideas for your job. Reading literature does not have to mean buying the latest ASHE Reader and slogging through like you are back in graduate school. Rather, it can look like reading *The Chronicle of Higher Education*, *Inside Higher Ed*, or *HuffPost College* on a daily basis. It could be asking mentors and colleagues for recommendations of seminal books or articles. It may mean reviewing peer and aspirational institution (your college or university has a list; ask for it) websites to see what other people are doing in your functional area. It might require considering business models or scientific theories that could be applied to higher education. Or, if you are like me, it could include making a list of books that you want to read each year, including works from higher education, business, psychology, or other related fields. Literature means many things these days, and books are only one aspect of that. Find the type of literature that works for you, and be consistent with your involvement with it. It will pay off when you have something to reference in a meeting or foundational information for a new idea.

Participating in Conferences, Institutes, and Webinars

This topic will come back around when professional development is discussed, but it is also important to note here that learning through attending and presenting at conferences, at institutes, and with webinars is a frequent option in higher education environments. These opportunities allow you to meet—in person or online—with colleagues around the region or country to discuss new and enduring topics in the field, exchange ideas, connect, and reflect. Sometimes these opportunities are free, but, more often than not, they come with a (substantial) cost. Keep these in mind as assets in informal learning, and I will come back to them in Chapter 6.

Engaging in Intentional Conversations

The final way to incorporate informal learning into your life is the most simple and frugal method: talking with purpose to people. This can occur on a daily basis and does not need any setup. You can do this with supervisors, supervisees, peers, mentors, students, friends, and strangers. You can do this on campus, at the coffee shop, in line at the grocery store, or over a meal. The only essential elements to this learning process are to converse with intentionality—to make the conversation thoughtful and meaningful—and keep the number of contributors small (maybe five or fewer) so that all participants feel they have time and space to contribute. The topic may or may not be directly related to higher education or be shared with someone in the field; in fact, you may learn more if you discuss education with those outside the field. I had this experience recently at a sports bar. I got into a heated debate about educational access with someone whose career was in business and who shared a much different philosophy than I did. The exchange was both frustrating and enlightening, and I am better for having had it because it allowed me to view educational access through a new lens, even if it is not one with which I agree. So, talk with purpose to people. It is a free and easy way to engage and to learn. Chapter 7 will focus specifically on ideas for networking or connecting.

Personal Stories

Lifelong learning is a process, literally and figuratively. It often involves both formal and informal learning processes, and it generally is a trial-and-error process to realize which learning methods work for you. Following are the stories of five individuals—Mat, Amber, Sandra, Laura, and Jeremiah—who do, or did, choose work in colleges and universities and how they practice lifelong learning through professional endeavors, personal experiences, or a combination of both. Read their stories to find how they holistically incorporate lifelong learning tactics into their lives, and open your mind to their suggestions of how you can practice lifelong learning.

Mat's Story

Lifelong learning is about capitalizing on opportunities and responding to the unexpected, even when it is extremely harsh, in order to create something positive. I am not convinced that lifelong learning is academic or formal. I believe that lifelong learning is simultaneously fun, painful, glorious, and sad. As such, everyone's life is full of pivotal moments that change an individual's course and direction forever. How you grow from those moments are your lifelong learning opportunities. It could be the birth of your first child, your first job out of college, or the first time you failed to accomplish a significant goal or dream. I have enjoyed, or endured, many of those life-altering moments. However, one such moment stands out because what started as a way to deal with pain, sorrow, and fear resulted in one of the most memorable life-altering experiences, and it permanently shifted my life's direction.

In 1995, I sat at my mother's headstone and wept. She had passed away four years earlier when I was 16. That morning is still very vivid, and I was explaining to her (via her headstone) that I needed to leave, to move forward, and to live my life. I was about to ride my bike 800 miles from Denver, Colorado, to Pocatello, Idaho, alone. I needed to take this risk, accept a huge failure, and return to a healthy and growing community in Pocatello where I was attending college. That was the last time I have been to my mother's headstone on my own. On that August morning, I was alone, scared, and lonely. I was also about to embark on what continues to be an amazing lifelong journey.

At the time, I only knew that I needed to move forward with my life. I learned more about who I was, what I aspired to be, and how to get there in the 10 days I pedaled across Colorado, Wyoming, and Idaho than I had at any point previous. The experience changed me forever by exposing a passion for outdoor education and outdoor leadership. I felt good about life and was ready to learn more, get outside, teach others, and improve my leadership skills. Upon arriving in Pocatello, I went to the Outdoor Program and asked for a job. Guess what? The Idaho State University Outdoor Program hired me, and so began my career in student affairs, higher education, and now politics. The successes (and failures) I have experienced in my professional and personal career hinge on three basic beliefs that I hold regarding lifelong learning.

There are three essential human skills that, in my opinion, help us capitalize on opportunity and capture the unexpected to ensure effective lifelong learning: embracing risk, accepting failure through personal forgiveness, and recognizing that others help us on our journey. In my case, my mother, through her death, inspired me to embrace risk, forgive myself for failing, and recognize that my success is contingent on my ability to cultivate a vibrant personal community.

Risk is the presence of potential loss. Accepting risk does not mean taking unnecessary risk. In fact, accepting risk means doing everything to reasonably and safely overcome it, because the potential gain is worth it. I am an outdoor programmer and professional mountain guide, and when I write about risk, people often assume I mean physical risk: falling in a crevasse, swimming in a dangerous rapid, or pushing through a very tight crawl space in a cave. However, the risk associated with lifelong learning is as simple as engaging in conversation with a perfect stranger on a bus, admitting that you do not know the answer to your students, telling someone you love him or her first, or setting a serious life goal when significant obstacles may impede your path. Embracing risk means stepping toward uncertainty, because you can see a path to personal success or, conversely, potential failure—all the while relishing the opportunity to learn.

Failure is an acceptable outcome. In mountaineering, success can be defined as not reaching the summit after doing everything possible in a reasoned and safe manner to attain it. Failure is getting yourself or others hurt or killed; reaching the summit is irrelevant to the process. Key words: *reasoned* and *safe*. Failure for a lack of effort, planning, or personal engagement violates the first principle of accepting risk and doing all that you can to overcome it. That is also known as laziness. Accepting failure is a cornerstone of lifelong learning. Even the most carefully calculated risk has an element of potential failure. The fact is that failure is often the best opportunity for substantial lifelong learning to occur. Again, as a mountaineer, I have failed to reach more summits than I have stood upon. As a professional, more of my ideas turn out to be duds than successes. As a friend and colleague, I have even been known to let someone down now and again. After all, I am human. The key to successful failure is to own it, reflect on it, apologize from your heart, and forgive yourself. Failing to succeed (on a mountain, in a relationship, at a job, in a college class, whatever it is) invites opportunity for growth. However, in cases of significant failure, often the biggest roadblock to growth is personal forgiveness. You have to be willing to forgive yourself for your failures, learn from them, and avoid them in the future. Trust me—you will have ample opportunities to fail at something else, and it is okay.

Accepting help from others is essential. How many times has someone provided you with a hand up, a shoulder to cry on, or words of support as you wrestled with a life challenge? I live 900 miles from my immediate family, but my "family" (those who are most honest and authentic with me) live all over the world. Success in any community depends on the ability to create and sustain meaningful relationships that matter to both individuals. Lifelong learning through relationships can be challenging. An authentic relationship means conflict, and conflict may take time and energy to resolve. An authentic relationship means hearing feedback that is constructive, being asked to take a risk for someone, being asked *not* to take a risk because of the impact it might have on someone, and being thankful for every experience with that person, good or bad. Relationships help us grow, allow for diversity in our lives, challenge our thinking, and help us expand our horizons through human interaction.

Lifelong learning should not always be fun. We all do something that in hindsight was not the correct decision, but our opportunity is to learn from it because moving forward is mandatory. In 1991, I was asked to call someone on Valentine's Day. I decided not to call that person, because I had rationalized that she would be there when I came home, and I did not want to be seen by my friends as anything but tough. Through my assumption, I risked *not* telling someone that I loved her on Valentine's Day. That risk resulted in a substantial failure, because my mother was not there when I came home. She had suffered an aneurysm and passed away abruptly. It took me four years, 800 miles, lots of tears, and the cultivation of a great community for me to forgive myself for taking that risk. Risk, failure, and our communities are absolutely essential for lifelong learning to occur. Remember that taking lifelong risk is different from ignoring obligations, but failure might occur either way. Forgiving oneself is essential to ongoing lifelong learning. Building and maintaining a community that challenges your perspective while encouraging responsible risk and helping you struggle through failure is essential. Lifelong learning is not passive, idealistic, or easy. It is sometimes difficult, dark, and isolating. However, it is absolutely necessary, and those who are intentional learners never turn back. So keep taking calculated risks, remember to forgive yourself for failure, and cultivate communities everywhere you go.

Amber's Story

Herbert Gerjuoy stated, "Tomorrow's illiterate will not be the man who can't read; he will be the man who has not learned how to learn." As knowledge becomes more abundant and easily accessible using technology, learning in the twenty-first century has more to do with what people can do for themselves by understanding how to direct and regulate their own learning. We also know that the number one factor in learning, regardless of cognitive ability, is motivation. Meaning, anyone who is motivated and understands how to manage his or her own learning has the ability to continue to develop over a lifetime.

For professionals working in higher education where learning is an inherent value of the organizations for which we work, embracing lifelong learning is an essential career strategy. Each of us has to ask, "What role does learning play in our personal development?" and "What does learning mean as a part of my professional identity?" Here is one story, one perspective on how a philosophy of lifelong learning can shape career strategies.

My personal and professional development has been an ongoing commitment and one that I have directed and maintained motivation for over the years. I state personal along with professional development because I believe awareness of self (personality, emotions, identities, values, and needs) is essential to learning and achieving success. I want to learn in every area of my life and challenge myself to gain a depth and breadth of knowledge. This philosophy allows me to see life as learning, a constant state of growth or the process of becoming.

I have always been very intentional and selective about the experiences I engage in professionally. As a woman, I felt it was important for me to gain credible academic credentials. I sought my degrees from three distinct institutions with reputations for excellence in student affairs. I also opted for degrees with science foundations rather than professional foundations (i.e., master of science over master of education and doctorate of philosophy over doctorate of education) because of the credibility they afford and the theoretical base they require. I worked throughout my doctorate, and although it may have taken me the full time to complete the degree, it was important for me to advance my career at the same time. As a learner, I knew I needed to keep one foot in the practitioners' world in order to be a better researcher and vice versa. There were certainly some negotiations to be made between work, school, and life, but instead of focusing on balance, I focused on blending. I accomplished personal, work, and school goals using a flexible schedule.

Although formal education has been a major strategy for my career, I cannot overstate the importance of the informal learning opportunities I created to build social capital and advance as a leader. Informal learning can be

summarized as the people and experiences that provide me with the opportunity to gain new knowledge, reflect, discuss, and practice.

Because there is no set curriculum or defined courses for informal learning, I took it upon myself to set up a development plan every year. I ask
myself, "What do I need to do to be a well-rounded professional and person?" and "What is my next career move, and what do I need to do to prepare today?" I review professional competencies and job descriptions and ask
mentors to help confirm what to focus on each year. The result has been a
combination of strategies that maximized every avenue I could access. I make
the personal and professional investment in the following learning strategies
every year.

A staple of my informal learning strategies has included contributing to
professional associations and campus initiatives. Joining committees, reading conference proposals, presenting, and taking on volunteer leadership
roles have allowed me to stay connected to the field and at the forefront of
developments. On campus, the roles help me understand how to be a good
partner in creating seamless educational environments and how institutions
work. In addition, I take on leadership roles in the community. Through
one particular role, I managed a team of 54 volunteers who lived across the
United States and Canada, gaining supervisory, budget, strategic planning,
and assessment experience. These opportunities broaden my skill set and give
me the ability to develop new skills while also working to contribute to the
community.

As I mentioned earlier, technology has put the world at our fingertips,
and we have access to more information than ever before. I read online via
Twitter and Flipboard because the content from policy centers, journals,
nonprofit agencies, and businesses gives me at least one or two compelling
arguments to consider each day. I find many of my best ideas that alter the
way I work and how I do my work better come from inspiration outside
of the field. The amount of information shared can be overwhelming, but
I have also learned how to speed-read. I recognize that even 15 minutes a day
exposes me to new ideas that can transform the way that I work.

I would be remiss if I did not mention the importance of people in the
evolution of my career and development. The ability to engage in meaningful relationships with others has enriched my journey beyond measure. There
are many people in my life who have acted as mentors, sponsors, supervisors,
and friends. I have a network of people on whom I can depend because we
have a reciprocal relationship built on trust and authenticity. Some people
have pushed and challenged me to know myself, some have been a place of
support during difficult times, some have opened doors to advancement, and
some have allowed me to mentor them.

Last, but not least, are my personal endeavors to love fearlessly, laugh often, knit, paint, run, wine taste, and travel. Every time I travel, I have learned something more about my resiliency, adaptability, and rigidness. Painting and wine tasting remind me to pay attention to the smallest of details. Love and laughter remind me there are always forgiveness, humility, and acceptance. The rich balance of play, relaxation, companionship, and adventure has kept me focused on a life as full of learning as I want it to be.

Sandra's Story

When I was preparing to graduate with my bachelor's degree, I decided that I wanted to be a university president. Once that decision was made, I asked a few trusted advisors, and among all the advice I was given, the two things that continually came up were (a) if I am going to take an administrative route, I'll need a lot of varied experiences, and (b) I have to get a PhD.

In terms of gathering varied experiences, I found that it could be quite difficult to accomplish that task within student affairs depending on the type of institution in which you found yourself. I spent the first seven years of my career at a large (more than 20,000 students) institution in very specific student affairs roles. Within those seven years I changed positions only once, so I basically had two very specific jobs, and both involved working directly with student organizations. After about five years of that, I knew that I was not necessarily going to fulfill my dream if I kept going down that path, so I eventually requested a change in my job description so I could at least begin to get new experiences. Thankfully I was granted that change, and even though my title didn't change, the new responsibilities were exactly what I needed to continue growing in the profession.

In addition to my professional experiences, I also sought out and/or embraced opportunities for growth and increasing responsibilities on the National Board of the Black Female Development Circle, Inc., my local chapter of the Order of the Eastern Star, and my local alumnae chapter of Delta Sigma Theta Sorority, Inc. Specifically, I was looking for opportunities to supplement the experiences I was not receiving at work, such as supervision, fund-raising, and project management. Although the organizations I was involved with completely fulfilled a personal desire to give back to my community, I made sure to be selective and intentional in where I spent my time so it could also help me learn more about the areas I needed to develop professionally. I am confident that the combination of professional and community leadership roles and experiences was extremely pivotal in helping me to land my current position. In my current role, I am able to oversee and supervise staff in many different departments, and the primary reason I was given the opportunity to do so is the varied responsibilities and experiences

I previously had. Those who knew only my two professional roles thought I would be in over my head when I told them about the position I accepted at my current institution, but that was simply because they didn't know all the other things I had been doing over the years.

As it relates to my academic pursuits, in all honesty, the idea that I *had* to get a PhD was quite depressing. I had no real desire to go back to school after getting my master's degree, and the idea of more student loan debt was less than encouraging. However, after considering my overall goals and the level of appreciation for advanced degrees within the academy, I decided that I did in fact need to get my PhD. Still, making the decision that you need a doctorate and actually going back to school to get it are two very different things. My original plan was to go straight through from master's to doctorate with no time in between, but once I got my first job, that proved to be a little more difficult than I thought it would be. I knew I would need professional experience to be taken seriously once I had my doctorate, so I started working with the plan to begin my doctoral studies part-time. Unfortunately, because of the amount of time my new job required (we all know the 24-hour nature of student affairs), my boss at the time was not supportive of my taking classes and working at the same time. Although I really liked my job, I made the tough decision to look for a new position where I would be able to pursue my degree, because it was *that* important to me.

Once I found a position that was a little more flexible, I began to take doctoral classes part-time. For the first two years, I took classes only over the summer, because working full-time and taking classes is not easy to do. However, after two years of that, I began to get antsy and frustrated because I had no desire to "waste" the next 10 years trying to get my degree. So, it was time to make another tough decision. Should I quit working and go to school full-time or try to go to work and go to school full-time at the same time? Again, I weighed all my options and decided that although it would be very difficult, the best thing for me to do professionally would be to continue to work full-time and at least attempt to pursue my degree full-time. Once I committed to my decision, I was able to work full-time and complete my degree within three years. It certainly was not easy, but I was able to dedicate the required time and energy simply because "I had to." Looking back, I can't really explain why I was in such a hurry to finish my degree, and if I had it to do all over again, I might do it a little (just a little) slower. But overall, I know I made the right decisions to gain the knowledge and experiences I need in the profession.

Now that I have my doctorate, a wealth of new opportunities has become available. I am invited to "have a seat at the table" more often, and I have also been invited to teach upper-division courses in leadership and women's studies. Through teaching, I continue my own learning and also add to the various experiences I'll need to achieve my ultimate goal. Looking to the future, I have begun pursuing opportunities for research and conference presentations. I believe this will help me to stay current in the field and contribute in meaningful ways.

By and large, I am dedicated to learning and growing as much as I can both personally and professionally. As times continue to change, there will always be new things to learn and new ways to do our jobs. Professional aspirations aside, it just makes sense to continue to grow and challenge yourself to be the best you can possibly be. That growth can be achieved only through intentional learning and development both in the field and in our everyday lives.

Laura's Story

At the age of 63, after successfully passing five rounds of group interviews, my mom began her third professional career, this time with Apple; this year at 64, she was promoted. When not finding, reading, and sending me books on civic engagement, Bill, my lifelong professional partner, coaches a middle school girls' softball team in Baltimore; he retired from Florida State University three years ago. And after a 44-year career in student affairs, my father recently retired from the University of Maryland and immediately started taking acting classes in DC; he just ordered prints of his head shot for upcoming auditions.

This reflection on lifelong learning comes from the lessons I have learned and the observations I have made not only from my life but from incredible role models who soak up life and live it to its fullest. So it follows that my first and most important thought on creating a life of learning is to surround yourself with people who reach for new ideas, experiences, relationships, and risks. My thoughts here can be captured in a simple question: Who challenges you to think?

Margaret Wheatley's writings introduced me to the concept of information as the scaffolding of our lives. Literally, the data we let "in" create the "formation" of who we are and who we will become. I had always believed in lifelong learning, but Wheatley's words clarified for me the nurturing, life-defining importance of seeking out and bringing "in" new relationships, knowledge, and questions to my way of being. This reflection shares how I strive to bring in newness to my life and why it is so important to me personally and professionally.

Becoming a lifelong learner is grounded in my personal belief that I exist through my relationships with others. These relationships bring new knowledge and ways of being into my life. Who I am is a result of the quality and diversity of my relationships. I can best understand our collective world through bringing individuals' stories into my mind and heart. I discover my best self through the continual process of integrating the bits and pieces of others that shock, awe, confirm, and amaze me.

Professionally, beyond accreditation standards and state governors' return-on-investment business models, we must understand the impact and outcomes of our work in order to be relevant in students' lives. To assume the professional degrees we received 15, 10, or even 2 years ago provide a complete picture of what we need to serve and develop students today is simply misguided. Relevance is what matters. And I can be relevant only when I am fully present and aware of current realities and possibilities. The beautiful truth in our work is that we are surrounded daily by students who have much to teach us about their lives. I often remind myself to take time to learn from those whom I seek to teach.

With this personal and professional motivation, there are three strategies I work on to bring new information into my life:

1. *Seek new sources.* Read the journals, blogs, posts, and publications of our profession, and complement this knowledge with sources that bring new and different ideas from unique contexts. *Fast Company* and *Good* magazines are great sources for our work from business and not-for-profit perspectives. The next time you pick up a book, look for something written by a faculty member on your campus. You may find not only a great read but an incredible way to start a conversation across the campus divide. Finally, social media offers an incredible opportunity to expand your sources of news and information. Following Al Jazeera on Twitter offers me a completely new perspective on current and global events.

2. *Attend and present workshops and trainings.* In addition to attending workshops, program sessions, and trainings, create, propose, and present them yourself. The catch is not to create them in areas you already know. Propose sessions in areas you would like to learn about and then engage colleagues in a collaborative learning process. Recently, three colleagues and I submitted a book proposal on a topic that we wanted to think about together. Once it was accepted, we had great motivation—and deadlines—to learn and write on the topic.

3. *Create learning relationships.* Similar to learning organizations, create learning relationships in your life. Be able to answer the question, Who do you think with? Develop a cohort of diverse thinkers who challenge and push each other's thinking, from one-on-one relationships, such as my colleague Carrie, who used to ask me at the end of each day, "What did you learn today?", to small groups of colleagues

with differing perspectives who engage in discussion without fear of disagreement. Build relationships rooted in curiosity about each other and our world.

Recently, researcher Trafton Drew from Harvard University replicated the selective attention test, better known as the Invisible Gorilla study. He super-imposed a photo of a gorilla on slides radiologists were reviewing for signs of lung cancer. Eighty-three percent of the radiologists looking at the slides did not see the gorilla. They weren't looking for a gorilla; they were looking for cancerous nodes. Scientists call this effect inattentional blindness. I remind myself of this study every time I am sure I am right. I wonder what gorillas I have not seen because I was so focused on seeing something else. It is easy to see and hear exactly what we are looking and listening for, and yet it is newness, difference, and the unexpected from which we will grow.

Without newness, our lives become stagnant. Our lives and our careers will not grow from a place of stagnation. To build a full career, you need to seek out new information to inform your work. Letting newness in can be scary. Newness shows up as difference, and difference brings change. This pattern can be fearful, for we know that the change process brings uncer-tainty and loss. Although learning involves a transitional time of unknowing and struggle, the payoff is worth the effort. If you need inspiration to lean into uncertainty, teach kids to read. Witness the struggle of uncertainty and worry of ineptitude with each new word, and experience the purest joy when they laugh out loud because they have read and understood a brilliantly silly Shel Silverstein poem. This same challenge of uncertainty and resulting joy is yours to discover daily.

Jeremiah's Story

I will be the first to admit that lifelong learning was not a concept I believed was applicable to me during my first couple of years as a student affairs professional. I had graduated magna cum laude with a degree in biology while being one of the most visible and involved undergraduate students on campus, a combination I believed to be quite an achievement at the time. Following graduation, I crammed three changes of clothes, a toothbrush, and a journal into my backpack; hopped on a plane; and spent the next 2 months sleeping in hostels, on trains, and on beaches in Europe and northern Africa. After growing up in a rural state, I was finally learning something about the world. Upon my triumphant return stateside, I moved into a housing co-op where I dutifully shared cooking and cleaning duties with 35 indivi-duals whom I would have never met were it not for our shared love of cheap rent. I jumped through the requisite hoops prescribed by my graduate program of study and ultimately earned a master's degree from a "top three" higher education program (nobody told me the arbitrary and irrelevant nature of rankings) before ultimately landing a great student affairs job on my first try, well before graduation. To that point, I had done everything expected of me, and I believed I was well on my way to becoming an overwhelming success in my chosen profession.

As I began my career, I was interested in making big decisions, dispensing advice, being important, and spending the minimum amount of time necessary at the entry level, but I certainly was not concerned with learning. Sure, I would pursue a doctorate someday, but only because I needed that stamp on my passport to validate my unique brand of student affairs brilliance. In my mind, I was a prodigy. I had already studied higher education through the lenses of history, philosophy, public policy, law, and org theory, so I was doubtful that further classes would make me any smarter than I was already. At this point, I believed I was knowledgeable enough to excel at my boss's job. Surely the only thing holding me back was the fact that I worked in a shortsighted profession that placed undue emphasis on *years of experience*. "Just give me the checklist, the catalog of buzzwords, and let me get older . . . and I'll be fine." This was my thought process as a young professional. I was wrong.

There is an exhausting amount of "Chapter 4" narrative (if that reference is lost on you, it won't be if you decide to pursue a doctorate) that fits here, but what's more important is what my journey from knowing everything to knowing nothing in 13 short years has taught me.

1. Learning as a professional is not about having a checklist, and it isn't always as simple as participating in a program, reading an article, facilitating a workshop, or attending a conference. It is not about what everyone else is doing, what someone has done, or what anyone thinks I should do. It's about *me*. This is my journey, and I get to chart my own path in the manner that best suits the kind of professional I am trying to become. For example, I read more business and finance literature than student affairs literature. Student affairs literature is not making me better right now. The other stuff is. For me, it's not about the content but about the framework. That is what I need to grow. Sure, I devote effort each week toward remaining current with regard to student affairs literature and thought, but it is not what makes me more effective.

2. Learning can occur only to the extent that I'm willing to challenge my own assumptions related to what I do and how I do it. Adlai Stevenson once said, "If we value the pursuit of knowledge, we must be free to follow wherever that search may lead us." Buying into this philosophy

ensures that I am going to be wrong more often than I would like. I take pleasure in being right, but the more often I am wrong, the closer I am to ultimately being right. It is a marathon, not a sprint. I do not have it all figured out. It wasn't until I owned up to that, that I was able to pursue what I really needed to be learning to advance our profession at the pace our world requires.

3. Learning is about always moving my thinking forward as an individual and as a professional. It is about refusing to get stuck in unproductive cultures or antiquated processes (and student affairs has plenty of both). Constantly moving forward requires me to *do* different. *Doing* different requires me to *be* different. *Being* different demands that I *think* differently. *Thinking* differently obliges me to *learn* more. And *learning* more demands that I am willing to ask incisive questions and to challenge my most foundational beliefs and long-standing practices and those of my chosen profession. This is why I read things outside of student affairs. I believe that irreverence is what facilitates progress. I do not find our literature to be irreverent, so it does not move me to think beyond where we are now. I want to do different; therefore, I need to learn something different.

4. Learning has been the by-product of experience. Experience matters. It has taught me more than all other things combined have. Although it would be possible for me to accumulate 13 years of experience only to still be bad at my job, I now know that without experience, I would definitely be bad at my job. I was incapable of leading a department when I finished graduate school. Actually, I was incapable of leading a department until about 6 months before I was responsible for leading one! Experience matters, and it is not just about *sitting in the chair* or *doing my time* but also about understanding the overwhelming nuance associated with leading, supervising, making decisions, and inspiring progress. The best professional development experiences I have had are my jobs. Nothing prepared me to be where I am more than where I have been. Experience matters.

I often find myself wanting to go back in time and talk some sense into the arrogant, green, 23-year-old version of myself. He was intelligent and had the potential to do great work, but he didn't know what he didn't know and was not yet willing to learn. I am thankful that he had some great mentors who were able to gently shatter his perceptions and introduce him to a world of ideas and alternate ways of thinking. He knows now that he will never be finished learning. Times change, and what was relevant yesterday is antiquated tomorrow. The process starts again each year. Such is the nature of life—and learning.

Chapter Summary

Mat, Amber, Sandra, Laura, and Jeremiah provide great examples of how you can incorporate lifelong learning into your overall career strategy. They also demonstrate that professional learning and personal learning are sometimes one and the same and that learning from others can be just as meaningful as firsthand learning experiences. This chapter gives you some ideas of how learning can be pursued, but the most important point is to know that learning, whether formal or informal, is a journey. And not one that should end—ever.

5

THE JOB HUNT AND EXTENDING YOUR EXPERIENCES

With contributions by Jasmine P. Clay, Kathy M. Collins, Juan R. Guardia, T. J. Jourian, Leisan C. Smith, and Jackie C. Thomas Jr.

> *Nothing ever becomes real 'til it is experienced.*
>
> —John Keats

> *The purpose of life is to live it, to taste experience to the utmost, to reach out eagerly and without fear for newer and richer experience.*
>
> —Eleanor Roosevelt

The Job Search

Although the process of lifelong learning is vital, if you are anything like me, you know there is also practical value in being able to put that learning into practice to assist others in their growth and development (and pay back your student loans and afford to support yourself). The job search process can be a time-consuming endeavor filled with self-assessment, anxiety, excitement, and a host of other emotional and logistical complexities. It is also a numbers game. For example, in my last job search after my PhD program, I applied for 46 jobs, participated in 12 phone interviews, visited 5 campuses for in-person interviews, and received 3 job offers. I like to think I am a solid candidate; the numbers also show you that I did not receive interviews with half of the places I applied. In fact, if you do the math, I was asked to interview with only 23% of the institutions to which I applied. That's real talk. I do not tell you this to discourage you. I tell you this because it is factual. You may need to apply to many jobs to find a job. So, let's discuss a bit about the job search process. Because whether it is your first time or tenth time on the market, the job search is quite the process.

Perusing Postings

The first aspect of the job search process is locating positions that are open and seeking applicants. There is no right way to look for job postings. There are, however, a few methods of searching that allow you to make the most of your time. Several online higher education job repositories exist that provide options of filtering your search by job type, location, and so on; the most popular sites include Higher Ed Jobs (www.higheredjobs.com), *The Chronicle of Higher Education*'s jobs site (http://chronicle.com/section/Jobs/61), *Inside Higher Ed*'s jobs site (http://careers.insidehighered.com), and http://jobs.studentaffairs.com. If you are conducting a regional or national search, these sites will be useful in seeing the majority of open positions. In fact, there are even sites like this for international options, including UniJobs, which host higher education postings in places such as Australia, New Zealand, the United Kingdom, Canada, Europe, Brazil, Argentina, South Africa, and the United Arab Emirates.

Realize, though, that colleges and universities have to pay to have their positions posted on these sites, and not all institutions have the desire or financial resources to market to a national, or international, audience. Thus, it is also important for you to review the human resources websites for any specific institutions in which you have a vested interest because institutions are required to post any position they have open on their own human resources job postings list. This even applies for internal-only positions that are posted for short stints of time.

Outside of websites, you can learn about postings from various e-mail lists, colleagues, your own connections and network (see Chapter 7 to learn more about building your connections), and search firms (for upper-level positions). Similar to "word of mouth," these tactics let individuals spread information about open positions to groups of people or individuals with whom they share a common interest. It is likely that your graduate program has an e-mail list for alumni where others connected to the program or institution can post open positions. National organizations and other professional development groups have e-mail lists or job boards where they send out opportunities. Colleagues may send things along to people they see as potential fits for open roles, and if you inform them of your search and how you are filtering it, your connections can keep an eye out for anything fitting your needs and notify you when opportunities arise. Finally, search firms are entities that not only head hunt for institutions for upper-level positions but also serve as resources for job seekers. You can sign up with search firms and send in your résumé in order to be on e-mail lists for postings for which they think you may qualify.

When job searching, you need to use as many of these information-gathering sources as possible. You need to peruse the postings on the repository websites. You need to spend time on human resources websites for institutions where your interest lies. You need to keep an eye out for mailing list e-mail. You need to inform your colleagues and connections of what types of roles and locations are on your ideal list. And, you need to sign up with search firms when you reach mid- to upper-level roles. Will that result in your seeing the same posting multiple times? Of course. But, it also helps ensure that you have as much information and, thus, opportunity as possible.

Finding Your Filters

As you peruse job postings, you will realize that there are hundreds of options that you could pursue. Even if you feel like your search has no limitations, it does. Seriously. You just may not have thought about it long enough yet to realize it. Why? Because there are places where you do not want to live. There are types of institutions you prefer. There are functional areas to which you are drawn. You probably have a range of salary and benefits that you need in order to live comfortably. You may need to consider loved ones and whether you need, or want, to live in proximity to them. See? There are things that will shape, or filter, your search. So, as you review those open position postings, consider the following as elements to help filter your search:

- Position
- Institution
- Location
- Supervisor and colleagues
- Salary and benefits (insurance, retirement, gym memberships, meal plans, professional development opportunities and funding, free academic courses, etc.)
- Opportunities outside the job
- Balance and quality of life
- Fit (with the position, staff, office, institution, location, etc.)

Narrowing your search by determining which filters matter most to you will help you focus on positions that more accurately meet your professional and personal needs.

Decoding Job Descriptions

Once you find position postings that fit your filters, it is important to critically assess what they are saying. Job descriptions are not always simple or easy to read. Often, they involve jargon or acronyms that may not be easily defined, they leave out key pieces of the everyday realities of the position, and they incorporate that elusive phrase "other duties as assigned." It is extremely important for you to learn how to decode job descriptions—your own and any to which you may be applying. So, how do you do that? Good question. First, print out (or bring up on your electronic device) a job description that appeals to you. Next, use the following suggestions to make notes on, and sense of, that job description.

Notice numbers. As you review a job description, notice numbers that are included. How many staff or students would you supervise? How many student groups would you advise? What, if any, is the size of the budget you would manage? Are the salary and benefits listed? What about the number of days of annual leave and sick leave? Numbers like this will clue you in on the scope of the job itself and the package that comes with it.

Pay attention to percentages. Some job descriptions will list job responsibilities with approximate percentages of how much time you will be spending on each aspect of the job. It may say 10% next to supervising staff, 25% next to advising students, 50% next to event planning and implementation, and 10% next to other duties. That tells you that the role is primarily centered on events with student support as a secondary focus. That may work for you. It may not. But, you need to recognize what the expectations will be about how you spend your time and decide if that will suit your work style. And if the job description does not list percentages next to the responsibilities, you should ask for them or for a general sense of where the majority of your time will and should be spent on a weekly basis.

Scope out similarities. Speaking of responsibilities, when you are decoding a job description, you need to determine how the listed responsibilities are similar to your past or current experiences. If it lists supervision, what supervision do you have on your résumé? If it talks about adjudicating conduct cases, when have you worked with conduct, crises, or personal counseling? If it speaks to extensive collaboration, what examples do you have of projects where you partnered with multiple constituents? In other words, how does your current portfolio of experiences and skills stack up against the job description responsibilities? You will need to assess this in order to write a solid cover letter, to prepare for any interviews, and to feel confident going into the job. It also allows you to reflect on how you will get to put theory and prior experience into further practice.

Glance for growth areas. Jobs should also, ideally, provide you with opportunities for continued growth. Look in the job description for a few areas with which you may have only tangential or no prior experience. Are these areas that you want to learn about? Will these areas fill gaps in your portfolio? What new skills or knowledge could you gain? This is important to think about for your own lifelong learning and also for elements to mention in the interview process that excite you about the job and serve as areas for development. It is also a way to assess where the holes may be between your experiences and skills and the job's qualifications and helps you to determine how to sell your transferable skills (see the following section) or your ability to be trained and continue developing.

Question the qualifications. Another key aspect of the job description is the qualifications section that lists the required and preferred qualifications for the ideal job candidate. This is where employers tell you what formal schooling, training, experiences, and skill sets they are looking for in the future employee. They want you to read it and determine if you "fit the bill" or not. A great piece of advice that someone shared with me once about the job search process has always stuck with me, and I think it applies well here. I was told to "never tell yourself no; let them tell you no." Wise words. If you are interested in the job but may not meet all of the listed qualifications, apply anyway. Let them tell you no. Because maybe you have something they did not even realize they wanted. Or maybe they see something in you that makes them want to bend their qualifications a bit. Now, I wouldn't suggest applying for a vice president role upon graduating with your master's degree; let's not get too outlandish. But, let them interpret if your graduate assistant years count as "years of experience" (personally, I think they should), if your undergraduate study abroad covers the "international education" requirement, or if your personal involvement with alumni clubs in the various cities where you have lived meets the "experience with alumni engagement" facet of the job.

Ask about what may be missing. Sometimes what is not listed is just as telling as what is covered in the job description. Is the salary range listed? Does it mention whether you will receive professional development funding? Are committee involvements specified? Are there any details about the "other duties as assigned" bullet point? Although job descriptions have only so much space to work with, if you want to know more about missing items in the description, it is okay to ask questions about them. Just be smart about to whom and when you ask those questions. It would not be the best idea to ask about salary when they call you to offer a phone interview. Rather, it is more appropriate to call human resources to inquire about some things before ever applying for the job, to wait until they call you with an on-campus interview offer to ask some of the financial details in order to not "waste" the interview, or to ask certain things in person during the on-campus interview process. Whatever you do, ask about things that are red flags or gut checks *before* you accept and start the job.

Rewrite to reflect the realities. Finally, it is vital that the job description reflect what you actually do within the role. Once you get into a job and have experienced an entire cycle (probably a year or so), you need to revisit the job description to determine if it is an accurate reflection of the job realities.

If it is, superb! If it is not, then you need to talk to your supervisor about rewriting the description to be more representative of what you really do and how much time you spend doing it. This will be helpful in the expectations people have of you, in how you manage those expectations, and in any future scenarios if and when you decide to look for another position.

Intelligent Interviewing

Let's pretend you have located an amazing job, decoded the description, and sent in all the required application materials. On the basis of your fantastic résumé and well-written cover letter that aligned your experiences and skills to the job description, you have now landed an interview. Congratulations! First things first in the interview stage; you will need to reflect and do your homework (those do not end with graduate school, sorry!).

Sell transferable skills. Reflecting on your transferable skills inside and outside of your formal job(s) is an important preparation method for interviews. This means getting out of your functional area box to consider how overarching skills can be sold to employers—things like supervising, advising, strategic planning, budget management, event planning and implementation, crisis management, assessment and data interpretation, presenting and facilitating, collaboration and partnership, social justice and diversity, and so on. Theoretically, you use these skills in every functional area. The question is whether you can market your experiences and skills to an employer in a functional area different from the one(s) in which you have worked in the past. Can you? If not, you need to think critically and holistically to consider how you may be able to assure a future employer that your transferable skills matter and will be useful in a new context.

This is particularly true if you are trying to switch functional areas. For example, if your current (and former) roles were within the area of residence life and you hope to find a new role in the union or student center, it will be key to show the employer how your facility management role with managing a residence hall and supervising resident assistants translates into an ability to oversee union spaces and work with student and community organizations. Or, if you want to switch from fraternity and sorority life to accountability/conduct/judicial, it would be important to showcase how your on-call rotation, crisis management, and conduct-hearing experiences in fraternity and sorority life have given you a foundation to work with the conduct/judicial area. In short, make it clear to the employer that even if you do not have direct experience in the functional area, you do have transferable skills that are precisely applicable to the new role.

Do your homework. Employers want to see that you are interested more in their job rather than in just any job. To show attentiveness, you have to do your homework. Yes, this is what it sounds like. You need to spend quite a bit of time learning about the institution, the division, the functional area, and the location. You should read websites, the local newspaper, the student newspaper, and so on. Talk to people you know who attended or worked at the institution. Remember that you are interviewing them as much as they are interviewing you, and you need to assess if the campus and community culture will suit you. And, if nothing else, analyze any materials that the employers provide prior to the interview. If they give you a list of people with whom you will be interviewing, look them up. If they tell you where you will be dining during the interview, check out the venue and the menu. But, please do not wait for them to provide you with materials. It is *your* responsibility to find information and use it in your interview responses and in your interview questions to the employer. Be prepared. Be informed. This "test" matters more than any you took in graduate school.

Also, do your homework on yourself. Although that may sound weird, what I am talking about is reflecting on your skills and experiences and considering how you would answer interview questions that you may face. If you have no clue what employers might ask, see Appendix B of this book for a list of sample questions that will shed a little light on what interview questions may arise in a phone, Skype, or campus interview.

Prepare for phone and Skype interviews. When you obtain a phone, or Skype, interview, you know you have made it into the smaller pool of candidates that the employer believes has the qualifications to do the job, at least based on paper. The first interview is a chance for the employer to determine if there is validity behind the words on your résumé and cover letter. It is also an opportunity for the employer to gauge if your personality could fit into the office and institutional culture. In my opinion, this is the most difficult component of the job search process. I think this because if the choice is a phone interview, it lacks key components of communication such as eye contact and body language, and if the employer goes with Skype, it creates potential issues with technology and the weird situation where you need to look at the camera on your computer to appear to be looking ahead or up, which means you really are not looking at any of the interviewers and, thus, still miss all the nonverbal communication aspects.

Regardless of the limitations, this first interview carries a lot of weight in the job search process. It is from this pool of candidates that employers will choose their final two to four candidates. So, you need to represent yourself well and make the best impression possible. Suggestions for enabling that include finding a quiet location to hold the call that has a strong phone or Internet connection, managing your time (do not spend more than 5 minutes on one question), and crafting insightful questions to ask the interview committee. After the call, follow up with a thank-you e-mail the same day to acknowledge your conversation and the time the interview committee took to learn more about you.

Gear up for campus interviews. If you are one of the two to four people whom the institution has chosen to invite for an in-person, campus interview, you need to gear up for a 1- to 3-day marathon interview and plan to answer similar questions for lots of different people. Schedules vary by position and institution, but here is a sample of what a campus interview schedule could include:

Student Activities Position

Candidate: ABC

Department of Student Activities, State University

Thursday, May 14–Saturday, May 16

Thursday, May 14

4:55 p.m.	Flight arrives
5:00–6:00 p.m.	Check in to hotel; free time
6:00–8:00 p.m.	Dinner at local establishment

Friday, May 15

8:00–8:45 a.m.	Breakfast at local establishment
8:45–9:00 a.m.	Travel to Student Union
9:00–10:00 a.m.	Search committee interview, Student Union Room A
10:00–11:00 a.m.	Student panel interview, Student Union Room A
11:00 a.m.–12:00 p.m.	Office and campus tour
12:00–12:30 p.m.	Benefits information
12:30–1:45 p.m.	Lunch at local establishment
1:45–2:00 p.m.	Break
2:00–3:00 p.m.	Presentation that is open to campus, Student Union Room C
3:00-4:00 p.m.	Peer colleagues panel interview, Student Union Room B
4:00–5:00 p.m.	Supervisors interview, Student Union Room B
5:00–6:00 p.m.	Travel to dinner and brief city tour
6:00–7:30 p.m.	Dinner at local establishment
7:30–7:45 p.m.	Travel to hotel

Saturday, May 16

9:30 a.m.	Check out of hotel
11:00 a.m.	Flight departs

See? It is a marathon. The reason for the extensive nature of the on-campus interview is to allow the employers and the candidate (i.e., you) to determine fit. They already think you are qualified for the job because they invited you to campus and are spending a chunk of money to bring you there (and they should be paying for the entirety of your trip!). The purpose of this level of interview is to figure out if you are a solid fit with the office and campus culture. Similarly, the on-campus interview provides you with the chance to get a feel for the job, your colleagues, the campus culture, and the community to decide if it would suit your needs and wants—if it is a fit from your perspective!

Along with showcasing your skills and experiences to multiple parties in this interview, your other goal is to show who you are. Let your personality shine through! Laugh. Make (appropriate) jokes. Talk about books you have read recently or TV shows and movies that you enjoy. Like I mentioned before, they already think you meet the qualifications, so now they are trying to determine who you are more so than what you can do.

The critical aspect of this interview from your perspective is to pay attention to details and ask good, informed, and (sometimes) pointed questions. This is when you watch how colleagues interact with one another and with students. This is when you pay close attention to nonverbal communication when people answer your questions to determine if they are speaking freely or "spinning" their answers. This is when you inquire about salary and benefits if the employer has yet to inform you of those. This is when you, tactfully, bring up any recent media attention the institution received. Again, you are interviewing the employers as much as they are interviewing you! After the interview, follow up with a thank-you e-mail the same day to everyone you met (yes, this takes time and effort), and send an actual thank-you card to both your point of contact and your potential supervisor.

Gaining Experience Outside of Your Job Description

Congratulations again! You landed an amazing job that will provide you with a breadth and depth of experiences and skills. Your job(s) will be the primary way you gain experience and skills. However, there are plenty of additional ways that you can achieve breadth and depth within the field of student affairs, specifically, and higher education, in general. Three options we will explore here are extending your experiences through serving on committees, volunteering, and having personal interests.

Serving on Committees

Committees are a fundamental approach to getting work done in higher education. There are committees within departments, across divisions, and representing the overall institution. More committees can be found within regional, national, and international organizations. Some are standing committees to handle annual programs or projects; others are ad hoc to deal with a specific issue. Committee assignments may be included in your job description, you might be able to choose which ones you join, or you could be "voluntold" or cajoled to serve on a committee. Regardless of the logistics, committees are a definite way you can extend your experience.

It may be helpful for you to seek out committee roles that allow you to explore skills and experiences that broaden what you may be gaining in your job. Never had experience with residence life? Ask to join a committee in that area or join a professional organization's knowledge community board that centers on that function. Want to learn more about fraternities and sororities? Inquire about retreat or awards committees on campus or get involved with an international headquarters with which you may have an affiliation. Interested in gaining facilitation or presentation skills? Submit or review sessions for campus, regional, or national conferences. And tell people what you are interested in doing. That way, they can keep you in mind when committee spots become available or can send you opportunities that may come across an electronic mailing list or through the grapevine.

Volunteering

Very similar to committee work, the work of volunteers, many times, helps higher education function. Individual offices and departments need extra hands on deck to make a large event happen. Divisions ask for volunteers to work institutional events like convocation and commencement. Regional and national professional organizations seek interns, committee heads, facilitators, conference proposal reviewers, and a host of other volunteer roles.

Offering to volunteer (i.e., work for free) may not always seem like the ideal use of your time; however, it is a surefire way to extend your experiences. You can do this on your own campus by asking to volunteer or intern in functional areas other than your own for an extended period of time (several weeks or an entire semester) or by offering your time and talents for one specific event with another function area. You can pursue opportunities through regional and national organizations by joining, volunteering to be a part of knowledge communities pertaining to any area that interests you, offering to serve on conference planning or volunteer committees, and facilitating conference sessions. Again, it is a good idea to tell others what kinds of volunteer opportunities you are looking for so that your colleagues can connect you with prospects that match the experiences that you are striving to attain.

Having Personal Interests

It is also important not to limit yourself to experiences within the realm of higher education. You can seek new experiences and skills through your personal interests as well. For example, travel is something I enjoy deeply on a personal level. I like exploring other cultures, places, and ways of thinking and being. On the surface this may not seem very useful to my career; however, travel provides me with experiences that allow me to question myself, to hear new perspectives, to see different things, and to expand my mind-set. All of those things are valuable to my work because they allow me to learn about others and myself and provide me with a broader view of the world and how it can work.

Other interests can have similar positive influences on your career. If you like to read, incorporate what you learned from those books into your work or use them as conversation pieces to connect to colleagues and students. If fitness is your thing, apply those concepts of discipline, resilience, and balance to your career. If involvement with community organizations and nonprofit agencies is how you spend your personal time, take the skills of organizing, serving, and fund-raising to your real job. The point is that your personal interests and what you gain from those interests can extend your career experiences in ways you never imagined as long as you think to apply those concepts and skills and then remember to sell them as transferable skills (see the earlier part of this chapter).

Personal Stories

Extending your experiences is something that may happen naturally; however, if you are intentional about having those experiences and seeking opportunities that add to your knowledge and skill set, you can utilize your job, committee work, volunteer experiences, and personal interests to their utmost capacity. Following are the stories of six individuals—Jasmine, Kathy, Juan, T. J., Leisan, and Jackie—who have figured out how to extend their experiences through a multitude of methods. They share how they have used committee work, volunteer opportunities, and personal interests to shape their own careers. Read their stories to find out how they gain knowledge and skills inside and outside of their formal positions in higher education. Hopefully, their stories will provide insights to how you can extend your own experiences.

Jasmine's Story

- "No" means "find another way."
- Take every opportunity that you can to learn.
- You are in control of your destiny.

These are three of the many success strategies that I repeatedly heard when growing up. As I reflect on my life and career experiences, I quickly realize that the lessons role modeled by my parents have affected every facet of my life, including those as a student affairs professional.

"No" means "find another way." Although this strategy never worked with my parents, it has helped extend my career experiences. I have learned the importance of doing my job well and how doing so can provide me with the opportunity to negotiate additional responsibilities. Again, I must stress that the key to this skill is excelling in your primary job responsibilities.

It is my responsibility to know myself, know the experiences that I want, and be willing to communicate these to my supervisor. In situations when I have expressed a desire for additional responsibilities, if what I want is important, I have learned that sacrifices sometimes have to be made in order to gain an experience. When I was presented with an opportunity to instruct a university course, university policies prevented me from receiving compensation in addition to my salary. I knew that the specific course was important to me and to the skills I sought to add to my professional résumé, so I made the decision, with the support of my supervisor, to instruct the course without compensation. Although this may not be desirable and/or feasible for everyone, I had to make a choice in the moment about the skills that I wanted to learn and how they would affect me in the future. Eight semesters later, I now realize this decision opened the door for me to have access to numerous additional opportunities, including presenting at faculty symposiums and writing for publications. Perhaps most important, it expanded my network of student interaction.

Finding another way also translates into trying something new or different when "no" might be my first response. I have learned that extending my experiences means taking risks and believing in myself. Countless opportunities have been presented to me, from serving as a classroom instructor, to serving on a campus search and screen committee, to copresenting a conference with the vice president for student life and dean of students. I've questioned why and wondered if someone would be better to take on a specific role, and I've thought that I did not have the time. One of the keys to extending my experiences is knowing and believing that I bring something that no one can offer.

Take every opportunity that you can to learn. I have learned that extending experiences can come from learning in a variety of places. One opportunity that I use to learn and grow is through seeking constructive feedback. This feedback allows me to know the areas where I need to seek guidance and experience to strengthen my skill set.

Search and screen committees have provided me with an opportunity to learn about departmental and institutional culture. As a committee member, I have learned the experiences that others believe are important and expect someone to possess to advance in specific areas of the profession. Being aware of these experiences provides me with an opportunity to gradually learn those skills. This follows the advice shared by a former supervisor, who encourages young professionals to "never stop job searching." I have made it a habit to save position descriptions for dream jobs. Doing so allows me to know what will be expected of me years from now and provides me with an opportunity to find ways to access these experiences throughout my career.

There are often countless opportunities to extend experiences on college campuses, if one views them as such. Stretching outside of my comfort zone by responding to requests to participate in campus-wide initiatives has created an opportunity to gain valuable experience and opened doors to future opportunities. A university-initiated, yearlong mentoring program led me to find ways to extend my experiences at other colleges and universities near my institution. You don't know what opportunities are out there until you take a risk and try something you might initially be hesitant about.

You are in control of your destiny. Don't wait for opportunities to come; make them. As an undergraduate student, I vividly remember a fellow student leader joking, "Jasmine has 27-hour days." Although I appreciated the recognition of my dedication to academics and extracurricular activities, this statement sent the wrong message to those around me. I did not and do not have any more time in my day than anyone else. What I was doing was important to me, and where you spend your time is an indication of what is important to you.

As a professional, I control my destiny by making time to extend my career experiences. Being involved in regional and national professional organizations, volunteering in campus offices, and staying current on trends in student development theory are a few ways that I control my destiny in student affairs.

The opportunities to extend your experiences in higher education are plentiful, and it is up to you to take advantage of them.

Kathy's Story

When I was preparing to go to graduate school, I struggled to find an assistantship. In fact, I started my master's program with no plan to pay for tuition and fees. Unfortunately, I had discovered student affairs late in my senior year, missing countless application deadlines. Then, I applied to only one school, where I was not offered any assistantships. As determined as I was to start my master's degree, I approached the start of classes rightfully concerned about my decisions.

As an undergraduate, I was a good student, a student athlete, and a resident assistant. As my first semester of graduate school approached, I was surprised when it was my athletic experience that provided me with a way to fund my master's degree. My first assistantship was working in the university's weight room. This position helped me network with staff in the athletic department. While I was working in the gym, the university's head swim coach began a search for a part-time assistant; the relationships that I had begun to foster in the weight room helped me land an interview. Because the part-time coaching role did not cover tuition, I sought out the athletic director to explore additional funding options in the athletic department. The athletic director offered me an assistantship overseeing the payroll process for the department's graduate assistants. Relieved that my networking and persistence had paid off, I was able to start my graduate course work thanks in part to the network that I had built by taking an alternative path—a sign of the career that lay ahead.

The second year of graduate school yielded similar results: no student affairs position. Desperation led me to contact most of the universities within a 70-mile radius of my graduate program regarding any student-affairs-related opportunities. The staff from only one school returned the call; they were looking to hire their first resident directors. After contemplating all of my options, I accepted the commute, and when I accepted the final offer, I was a female hall director in an all-male residence hall.

Fast-forward 20 years. The experiences in the weight room, on the pool deck, and in the all-male hall were the beginning of a successful career that is still taking shape. Over the past 20 years, not only have I worked in residence life, but I also continue to take advantage of opportunities throughout student affairs. Thanks to hard work, strong mentors, and wonderful colleagues, I have been able to obtain a broad skill set shaped by networking, chance, perseverance, and sometimes just plain luck.

Along this incredible, sometimes alternative, career path, two pieces of advice stand out as guiding principles. My graduate advisor at Shippensburg University provided counsel to me during my first professional job search. While I was struggling with the geographic location of a particular position, he wisely shared that I "was not always going to be where I wanted to be; I was going to be where I needed to be." These words have proven true as I have navigated my career. Throughout my career, I have worked in four states at multiple institutions ranging in size from 1,200 to approximately 50,000 students. I have held progressively responsible positions in athletics, housing and residence life, and student activities. Most important, every place I have worked led me to the position I hold today. In fact, I sit where I do today because I am exactly where I need to be.

The second piece of advice that made a significant difference in my life came from a mentor whose career path propelled him toward a college presidency. I asked him what I should do to move ahead in student affairs. Without hesitation, he advised, "Do the jobs that no one else wants to do." When I asked for clarification, he stated that I needed to become the "go-to person," to represent the department and division on university-wide committees. In other words, I needed to serve my colleagues in a different way. The learning was about serving on the committee, not simply leading them. Through experiences that included a campus-wide shared governance committee and a task force that examined a university's values, I built relationships, learned from high-level decision makers, studied the marshaling of resources, and completed university-wide projects.

Navigating a career path that led to my becoming the director of one of the largest housing operations in the country has not always been easy. I have been turned down for more jobs than I accepted, I took seven years to complete my doctoral degree, and I have made a lot of mistakes. But most important, I have never given up. I kept applying for jobs, I persisted through the dissertation, and I learn every day from my mistakes. Perhaps not getting an assistantship early in my career was exactly what I needed to jump-start my career on the right foot.

I update my résumé every 6 months. While updating the document for my current position, I noticed that the titled positions nicely fill up the most space, and the other experiences complement the document and finish it off. The time spent in the weight room, on the pool deck, and on the additional committees, task forces, and so on has provided excellent growth opportunities. When I am asked about career advice, I tell people that it is important for them to coordinate their career path with supervisors, mentors, and colleagues. Remember that your professional development is ultimately up to you. Make the most of the opportunities that are presented to you, create opportunities, and "do the jobs that no one else wants to do."

Juan's Story

As a Latino, first-generation college student, I attended Miami-Dade Community College for two reasons: the opportunity to live at home and the ability to assist my family personally and financially. I then transferred to Florida State University to complete my undergraduate degree. That initial move from home opened many doors for me, and since then I have been employed at and attended institutions in Virginia, Iowa, and, currently, Illinois. The importance of leaving that "safe place" has afforded me personal and professional experiences that I do not believe I would have obtained had I stayed in my home city of Miami. I highly suggest professionals be open to opportunities away from one's home and out of state because it can benefit one greatly.

In my current position as assistant vice president for student affairs at Northeastern Illinois University, I oversee the Angelina Pedroso Center for Diversity and Intercultural Affairs; it is home to the African/African American, Asian/Global, Latino, LGBTQA (lesbian, gay, bisexual, transgender, queer, questioning, and ally), and Women's resource centers. Previously, I was the director of the Center for Multicultural Affairs at Florida State University and also worked in the Office of Diversity Programs and Services at George Mason University. My specialty in the field has always focused on multiculturalism and social justice. It has always been my passion to educate students and members of the campus community on issues of inclusion and pluralism and how those concepts contribute to one's personal and professional development.

Several of my mentors, however, advised me to gain experiences outside of multicultural affairs to broaden my skills, abilities, and talents so that I would not be pigeonholed into one specific student affairs functional area. With that in mind, I have continually sought opportunities that add to my toolbox. Over the course of my career in student affairs, I have made it a point to become involved in a variety of experiences that complement my formal positions. As such, I have volunteered in a variety of student affairs areas to provide me with the generalist perspective. I have interned with university housing, served as a conduct or judicial hearing officer, and taken students abroad to Costa Rica and Guatemala. In addition, several committees I have participated on have expanded my own learning about such things as public safety, strategic planning, the advancement of fraternity and sorority life, student government, and campus and community civic health. Because of these experiences, I have gained a great deal of knowledge of student affairs areas not directly linked to my current area of multicultural affairs as I move toward my aspiration of becoming a vice president for student affairs.

My volunteer involvement with national associations has allowed me to gain valuable experiences from colleagues from across the country. My involvement began with the American College Personnel Association (ACPA). Through ACPA, I have served as Latino/a network cochair and research award coordinator and on three convention-planning committees. I am also involved with the National Association of Student Personnel Administrators (NASPA). Through NASPA, I served as a NASPA Undergraduate Fellows Program mentor and Latino/a knowledge community cochair, and I am currently on the editorial board of the *Journal of Student Affairs Research and Practice*. I am also involved with the LeaderShape Institute, which has allowed me to further my love of leadership programming and to engage with students from campuses across the country as they explore their leadership identities. I cannot stress enough the importance of volunteering in any national association and organization; it provides the individual with invaluable involvement experience and collegial relationships that transcend annual conventions.

As an undergraduate, although I was involved in various student organizations, I was not a member of a fraternity. During the spring semester of 2005, I joined Phi Iota Alpha Fraternity, Inc., as a doctoral student; the fraternity has a membership intake process for college graduates and professionals. Becoming a fraternity man has afforded me the opportunity to become involved in several professional development projects, including serving as an Interfraternity Institute facilitator and in various volunteer positions from director of public relations to the current chair of the National Association of Latino Fraternal Organizations (NALFO). NALFO is the national council representing 20 Latino/a fraternities and sororities with a membership consisting of over 25,000 undergraduates and alumni. I have also volunteered regionally and nationally with my own fraternity.

Teaching is important to me, and I believe it is my responsibility to educate the next generation of students. I have been fortunate to serve as an instructor to both undergraduate and graduate students. Teaching graduate courses as an adjunct faculty member in the Florida State University Higher Education/Student Affairs program, such as student development theories and diversity in higher education, has allowed me to translate theory into practice for future student affairs practitioners. One of my favorite moments was when I had the opportunity to cocreate an undergraduate student affairs leadership course. This introductory course offers practical activities designed to familiarize students with the theories, organizational structures, and issues, trends, and challenges of the student affairs profession.

Overall, I have benefited personally and professionally from extending my experiences above and beyond my on-campus positions. My fraternal involvement has provided me opportunities to discuss how ritual and creed play an important part in fraternal administrators' and students' personal and professional development. Teaching has allowed me to extend my professional experiences into the classroom. These opportunities, coupled with presenting at national conferences, serving as a consultant in my professional area, and speaking at various campuses, have allowed me to connect with colleagues across the country, opened doors for me, and helped me grow personally, socially, and professionally. In turn, all of these experiences have allowed me to become a better, informed, and dedicated student affairs professional, for which I am thankful.

T. J.'s Story

Like many who join the student affairs field, I know my undergraduate experience was a major influence in that decision. At Michigan State I participated in a lot of activism and leadership with various communities of students bent toward social justice advocacy. In joining the field, I hoped to support and empower students in continuing to do social justice work with them. Currently, I am a doctoral student with aspirations to teach multicultural competence courses for future student affairs professionals, and I take opportunities to expand my skills and experience as a social justice trainer.

Before going back to school, I worked professionally in two student affairs realms: residential life and LGBTQ work. Being a pansexual-identified trans* person of color who had been an international student, I was drawn to combating racism, sexism, genderism, heterosexism, and ethnocentrism as they manifest in these two areas. Unsurprisingly, after the first few months as a residence director, I gave the day-to-day administrative and crisis management aspects of the position permanent residence on my to-do list, and they were not about to make room for anything else. More unexpected was the amount and especially sources of institutional resistance and distraction I came across within the LGBTQ office. I came close to giving up and leaving higher education, because I was not doing the sort of work that I thought I was being hired for in the second role, judging from my interview and the recruitment materials. Undoubtedly, I was a bit more naive at times than I am comfortable admitting.

If I was going to sustain myself as a person and a professional in the field long term, I needed to extend my experiences beyond what was minimally required of my job. Both times, I employed a three-tiered approach that helped me stay grounded, committed, and provided me with skills and practice that moved me to my next chapter. The three tiers or steps can be summarized as follows:

1. What is immediately accessible within my formal position and office?
2. What are division-wide or campus-wide opportunities to get involved in?
3. What I can do outside of the campus boundaries both within and outside of higher education?

I'll expand on how I used each of these tiers in (a) my role as a residence director looking to get back into LGBTQ work and (b) my role as a program coordinator in an LGBTQ office looking to get into a PhD program to become a faculty member at a master's-level higher education program.

1. Immediately accessible

   a. Co-led a task force with staff and students on creating a gender-neutral housing policy for the department; reached out to and connected with the LGBTQ living/learning community in my complex; attended student-led queer and social justice events in my complex; assessed the building for gender-neutral restrooms; facilitated RA trainings, staff meetings, and classes that focused on or included social justice content; joined department committees like Professional Education and Training and Professional Staff Recruitment, Training, and Selection.

b. Worked with my direct supervisor on a research study looking at where and how LGBTQ student leaders access support; mentored two undergraduate students from the campus queer organization interested in the student affairs field, and a graduate assistant already in a master's program; participated in program evaluation and assessment practices; facilitated sessions on intersexuality and asexuality, topics that required my own research and self-education.

2. Within campus

a. Attended events put on by the queer student groups and office, as well as the groups serving and run by students and staff of color; got involved in the Queer People of Color and Men of Color groups; joined the Presidential Commission of LGBT Equity and the Divisional Diversity Committee; cofacilitated a weekend-long social justice retreat for students; and joined the advisory and participation selection committees the following year.

b. Cocoordinated the Transfer Orientation Committee, exposing myself to different competencies, student populations, and arenas than what I was used to; joined a variety of committees focused on diversity programming and education; connected with faculty that I thought did interesting work, exposing myself to their research and classrooms whenever I could, particularly if they taught graduate students; attended events put on by graduate student groups to reengage in academic and intellectual ways.

3. Off campus

a. Joined and participated in ACPA and NASPA groups and committees, including contributing to some of their newsletters, and attended the Social Justice Training Institute and various higher education and social justice conferences whenever I had the means.

b. Moved into a leadership position within NASPA; joined a regional Gay, Lesbian, and Straight Education Network board; got involved in the city's LGBTQ youth program as a volunteer and assisted the program's coordinator around trans* education; continued presenting at regional and national conferences, utilizing more and more empirical research, particularly on intersectionality; conducted trainings and spoke at various campuses around the country, allowing me to interact with a wide variety of institution types and students; read.

Throughout these three tiers, I looked for balance of responsibility, opportunities that didn't involve my professional role or campus affiliation, and experiences and contacts that would assist me in moving in the directions I wanted to next. The mixture of levels of responsibility (from coordinating initiatives to merely showing up as an observer or participant) allowed me both to parse out my time in a healthier way and to access some spaces for the purpose of my own learning and professional networking. The opportunities that allowed me to take off my campus administrator hat expanded my networks and perspectives beyond the confines of higher education and sustained personal interests that my jobs did not offer.

I purposefully chose projects that I felt inexperienced in, as those opened up new doors in moving forward. Although at times these choices left me feeling vulnerable and even anxious, they pushed me in ways I could not have imagined, made me more well-rounded, and increased my capacity to think through multiple lenses. I remind myself of this now as the research assistant for a faculty member who does quantitative work. As someone who finds it second nature to think qualitatively, I find that this experience forces me to shift ways of thinking and exercises inert areas of my brain. It is similar to folks exercising different muscles of their body or trying out new trainings. It is fairly tempting in this field to do what we know, lest we admit we do not know everything, thus sacrificing innovation and growth.

It was the combination of all of the above rather than any one committee or type of work, and the intentionality of balancing different priorities, identities, and needs, that helped me get the kinds of experiences that I wanted to view myself as a holistic professional and person. Many times I have overextended myself, and continue to do so, or alternately feel isolated and pigeonholed, so I just go back to asking myself whether something that I am doing is contributing to that balance or throwing it off. Which of my many hats and identities is not getting nurtured or challenged or given a break? Time to refocus.

Leisan's Story

Ten, or maybe even five, years ago, if someone had told me that I would one day be the director of an LGBTQ Center (nonexistent until three years ago) at my alma mater, I would have laughed. Now, when I look back over my experiences, I am clear that all of my work- and nonwork-related experiences have added to what I have to offer in my position as a student affairs professional. I am clear that, unknowingly, I began to lay the groundwork for my journey in student affairs and, more specifically, my work in and love for the concepts of diversity and inclusion a long time ago.

When I first saw the job posting for my current position, I knew it was my dream job. I was not sure if my previous job experiences would lead others to see me as a strong candidate, but I knew that I had what was needed to do the job well. I looked back at all of my previous positions and activities I had been involved in outside of work and discovered that most of them showcased my ability not only to work with diverse populations but also to advocate for them.

Student involvement as both an undergraduate student and a graduate student is an important aspect to showcasing your ability to be able to do well in a career in higher education. However, being an active student and graduating from college does not, of course, guarantee immediate employment at a college after graduation. All of the jobs I have had leading up to my current position have related to education in some way. When examining them more deeply, I realized they all involved advocating for a specific group of people, which is a great trait to have in student affairs.

Because of my substantial involvement in the African American Cultural and Resource Center as an undergraduate student, I was able to obtain a full-time staff position as a program coordinator with the center right after graduation. In this position, I oversaw a program for first-year, mostly first-generation African American students. Although I held this position for only a little over a year, this first full-time staff experience in student affairs helped to lay my foundation in higher education. It was also during this time that I pursued membership into a historically Black Greek letter organization. The mission of the sorority I joined is to enhance the quality of life within the community and focuses on public service, leadership development, and education of youth. Thirteen years in this organization has provided me with valuable leadership experience, and I have been able to use the skills learned and implemented in my sorority to highlight my leadership abilities when applying for jobs in student affairs. I have held several officer positions including treasurer and undergraduate chapter advisor on two college campuses. As an advisor, it was my responsibility to oversee bringing new women into the organization and help them learn how to run a meeting and function as a student organization. These experiences were valuable because I had the opportunity to work with college-age students and help them in their development as a leader.

A few years later when I decided to attend graduate school, studying educational foundations (back at my alma mater), I had another opportunity to work in a student affairs office, this time in the Women's Center. Although the work I did was focused on a specific population, being a part of the Women's Center afforded me the opportunity to focus on different aspects of diversity. I also had a chance to establish myself back on campus in a new role. These connections would help when I would later apply for the director position in the LGBTQ Center.

My personal interests have also been critical in preparing me for my current position. I have been a member of a local women's choir for about 10 years. The great thing about this choir is that part of its mission includes a dedication to social change. We often sing what I would call social conscious music. Music is something I love, so I have been able to do something I love while also having the opportunity to serve on committees that have dealt with diversity and inclusion in a very grassroots way. I was able to use these experiences when talking about the work I've done around diversity in my interview for my current position. Since obtaining the position, I have been able to link my university work with the work of the choir on several occasions.

To stay active in my current position, I have found that connections with other colleagues and departments at the university are vital. This is true for a number of reasons. The first reason is the importance of and the increase in conversations around intersectionality. Regardless of what specific population our office doors say we serve (LGBTQ Center, Multicultural Center, Women's Center, etc.), our students come to us with their full identities in tow. Although it might be our job to focus in on the identity on the office door, it is our responsibility to help our students become strong in who they are. This cannot be done well in isolation. Our office often collaborates with other student affairs offices so that we have a working knowledge of the multiple identities our students bring in the door. These collaborations allow me the opportunity to work with other populations, which helps to strengthen my experience and level of expertise in student affairs. Second, connections allow me to interact with students who may not come into the LGBTQ Center. This has been especially true for students of color. Although I myself am a woman of color, that does not automatically mean that students of color will gravitate toward my office. Because of this lack of exposure to students of color, I make sure to attend events on campus aimed at students of color, I volunteer for activities other offices are having, and I often sit on committees out of my direct functional unit. This strengthens my experiences and allows me to sell myself to any future jobs as someone who is not pigeonholed into just LGBTQ work. The third reason connections are key is they challenge me to continue to grow and keep other doors open for me. Although I love the work that I do, I may decide that I would like to do something else in student affairs. The connections and experiences I get from connecting with other departments keep my name out there and give me other experiences to refer to should I choose to apply for another position.

A job in student affairs is not normally one that you hear kids rattling off that they want to do when they grow up. However, now, there does seem to be an increase in people figuring out that this is a path they are interested in once they enter college. Most of the student affairs professionals I know were drawn to the work because of what they witnessed and experienced when they were college students. We are folks who love working with people, students specifically, and are often passionate about some aspect of diversity. It can be difficult to get a foot in the door in higher education, but using our undergraduate experiences can often be the way to showcase our qualifications. In addition, having other life experiences is important, and being able to relate them to student affairs is even more important. As a future student affairs professional, you should focus on your passion, the jobs you take (until you land your dream student affairs job), and the activities you participate in to help prepare you for your future.

Jackie's Story

I entered the field of higher education as an eager student affairs professional who wanted to learn as much as I could about the workings of the college and university. My eagerness to learn was fueled by my goal of becoming a college president. I remember taking a course in my master's program that introduced students to the different functions within a university. It was, by far, my favorite course in graduate school! For an entire semester, we learned about the roles and functions of areas like student activities, housing, multicultural affairs, new student programs, international programs, academic advising, financial aid, athletics, and student judicial affairs. After taking this course, I was certain that I wanted to be a college president.

As I thought about what it would take to become a president, I realized that there were a variety of opportunities, skills, and experiences that I would need. I remember being in my master's program and wanting to gain as much experience as possible. So, in addition to my 30+ hour a week graduate assistantship in student activities, I served as a judicial officer, cotaught a first-year experience course, participated in several committees, and planned our annual visiting days for prospective master's and doctoral students. I found that the more involved I became, the more I learned about different aspects of the college and university.

The "I want to learn it all" mentality transferred over into my professional career as well. After graduating from my master's program, I spent the first part of my career working in residence life. My first job right out of graduate school was a live-in position responsible for overseeing a residentially based retention program that focused on guiding, supporting, and mentoring 250 at-risk, first-year students. This was a great first job because not only was I able to better understand residence life (I had never worked in housing), but I was also able to learn a lot of the skills needed to successfully run a campus program. I gained experiences in strategic planning, facility management, staff supervision, research and assessment, training, event planning, grant research, and budgeting (all essential skills needed by college presidents). I also made it a point to join professional associations, present at conferences, be involved in departmental and campus-wide committees, and continue to find innovative ways to educate, encourage, and empower college students. In addition to working in housing, I also started a 501(c)3 nonprofit organization that focused on leadership and youth development in Houston. Not only did this experience complement my work in housing, but it also taught me one of the most important skills I have to date: the ability to fund-raise.

About two years into my first job, I realized that I wanted a different experience. Although student affairs was my entry into higher education, I became more interested in the role that academic affairs played in student success. So, in addition to working as a housing professional, I also served as an adjunct instructor for our campus's First-Year Experience (FYE) course. I really enjoyed teaching the FYE course because the focus was not subject specific. My job was to teach students a variety of academic, personal, and professional strategies that would help them be successful. My experience with this course fueled my interest in student motivation and retention. So, at the end of my second year of full-time employment, I decided to quit my job, take a graduate assistantship, and pursue a PhD in educational psychology and individual differences.

While working on my doctorate, I learned that most college presidents became presidents by way of academic affairs. Therefore, it was important that I found a way to gain the experience needed to be successful in academia. Throughout my doctoral program, I served as a teaching assistant for a master's-level course, served as an adjunct instructor for the FYE course, and conducted research on student persistence and retention.

After I completed my doctoral course work, I accepted an assistant professor position at Lone Star College–Tomball, teaching our College Success courses. As soon as I stepped on the campus, I wanted to find a way to get involved. I currently serve on several local, campus-based, and statewide committees, as well continue to conduct research, write, and publish.

In my classes, I talk to my students about the importance of setting goals. As a matter of fact, the Lone Star College System has adopted an initiative called the "Best Start," which focuses on four steps that will lead to student success: set a goal, make a plan, get connected, and stay involved.

One evening, I was reflecting on the four steps, and I decided to apply them to my own life and career.

Set a goal. I told myself that I would be a college president by the time I was 40 (pretty optimistic, I know). I wrote this goal on a piece of paper and stuck it on my bedroom mirror. I also told my wife, best friend, close colleagues, and supervisor, so that they could all hold me accountable to this goal.

Make a plan. I realized that I needed a plan for how I was going to become a president. So, I sat down and created a flowchart that outlined two different paths I could take (student affairs versus academic affairs) to become a college president (see Figure 5.1).

In addition to creating this flowchart, I wrote down all of the major skills and experiences I thought I would need to become a college president. The following are a just few that I listed:

Figure 5.1 Jackie's Career Flowchart. This chart shows how Jackie plans to move through his career and reach his end goal.

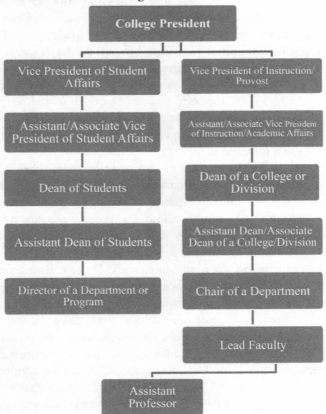

- Attain a doctorate (not a must, but preferred)
- Develop strong leadership skills
- Learn staff supervision
- Gain budgeting experience
- Be relatable
- Be able to network and fund-raise
- Be able to speak well
- Be able to motivate others
- Be able to keep people invested
- Be able to make tough decisions

Underneath each skill, I wrote down all of the experiences I had that were related to that skill. I also included experiences that I needed to strengthen that particular area. Finally, I began to brainstorm about how I could get these experiences in my current position at Lone Star College–Tomball.

Get connected. After I listed out all of the skills I needed to serve as an effective president, I thought about the people I should connect with who could help me to achieve my goal. I am fortunate to have a very supportive department chair, dean, vice president, and president. They help me find a balance in my work, as well as identify opportunities that will help me grow as a professional. I also am blessed to work with amazing students, faculty, and staff (whom I learn from every day).

Stay involved. I thought about how important it is for me to stay actively involved with my campus and community. I wrote down a list of all of the committees and organizations I am involved with. As I reviewed each of them, I made a commitment to be an active participant. I didn't want to be involved in something and not contribute. I've learned that if I am engaged, these professional growth opportunities are extremely beneficial.

After I finished everything, I realized that utilizing the Best Start steps helped evaluate where I was going professionally.

I have always considered myself to be rather strategic. I believe that the professional choices I make now will impact the opportunities I get later. Therefore, every experience I have sought out and every career decision that I have made have been connected to my goal of becoming a college president. These experiences guide my work and will ultimately shape my career.

Chapter Summary

The stories of Jasmine, Kathy, Juan, T. J., Leisan, and Jackie are representations of how you can extend your experiences as one tactic to your overall career strategy. They exhibit how knowledge and skills can be obtained and reinforced through a variety of experiences, including but surely not limited to the actual job for which you get paid. In fact, their stories speak to the utilization of experiences outside of their formal roles and pertaining to their personal interests. Extending your experiences is about using all of your experiences—at the institution, in professional organizations, with the community, and inside your home—to shape your mind-set and skill set and to explore paths that you may not have first considered as options. This chapter gives you some illustrations about how you can take your experiences to another level. The challenge now is to actually do it!

6

PLANNING FOR PROFESSIONAL DEVELOPMENT

With contributions by Allison Crume, Jomita Fleming, Jordan Hale, and Robert "Jason" Lynch

Nothing happens until you decide. Make a decision and watch your life move forward.

—Oprah Winfrey

My future depends mostly upon myself.

—Paul Robeson

It Is Your Responsibility

The term *professional development* is a bit misleading. Upon hearing or reading it, you may believe that it means the profession is here to develop you. That is not actually true. Your supervisor does not have to focus on your growth and learning. The institution where you work may or may not believe in spending time or money on training you in new and different ways. The overall profession has thousands of individuals in it and more on the way, so why should it give time and attention to you? Here is the real deal: It is your responsibility to develop as a professional. *Your responsibility.* Instead of *professional development*, the term should really be *self-development in your profession*, because that is where the responsibility lies.

This may seem daunting. I get that. And I am not saying that you will not work for places and people who genuinely care about offering opportunities for you to strengthen existing knowledge, skills, or experiences or acquire new ones. The point is that if you do not take stock in developing yourself, why should other people?

Navigating Professional Development Options[1]

First things first: You need to take an inventory of your knowledge, skills, and abilities. Review your résumé and your job description. Are these clearly articulating your current role? Do you conduct self-evaluations annually? No? Well, start now! One of the tools you can use for self-assessment is the *Professional Competency Areas for Student Affairs Practitioners* (ACPA and NASPA Joint Task Force on Professional Competencies, 2010). These competencies can help you articulate skills gained while providing a framework for new areas of learning.

The next step is thinking about your professional goals. Where do you want to be in 1 year, 5 years, or 10 years? (See the questions in Chapter 3.) Find one or more "dream job" postings that excite you. Review the dream job description and highlight the required skills and expectations. Reflect on what it is about this role that motivates you. Consider your current job and identify how you may be able to gain the required experiences for your dream job on your campus.

Once you have your materials pulled together, it is time to compare your résumé with the skills and expectations required for your dream job. Identify areas of learning and the specific competencies you need to be eligible for the dream job. Reflect on your network; reach out to people who hold positions similar to your aspired role. Spend time talking to them about their journey and listen to any advice they have. Themes will emerge that provide you with objectives, which will help create an individualized professional development plan.

Once you understand the competencies and goals, you will need to identify the methods needed to achieve those skills. Remember to think about your current institution and what opportunities exist. Talk with your supervisor about your goals; maybe you can participate in trainings or serve on a committee. Take advantage of the human resources department's trainings and professional developments offered through your division or department. Connect with colleagues to share suggestions for workshops. If this is a gap at your institution, consider helping to spur on an initiative.

Once you have exhausted all your in-house options, look to the field at large. Joining at least one student-affairs-related professional association will benefit you immensely. Professional associations serve, advocate, and support student affairs through the resources and opportunities they provide. State, regional, and national conferences offer you spaces to gather, connect, and share ideas. For some professionals, membership in a professional association directly linked to their specific area is most helpful. Keeping informed and educated is important in our ever-changing field. Several professional associations publish peer-reviewed journals such as *The College Student Affairs Journal* (Southern Association for College Student Affairs), the *Journal of*

College Student Development (ACPA), the *Journal of Student Affairs Research and Practice* (NASPA), and *The Review of Higher Education* (Association for the Study of Higher Education).

Several resources exist for you to stay in touch with current research and trends. *The Chronicle of Higher Education* is as an important daily read. Many student affairs divisions, student affairs graduate programs, and campus libraries have subscriptions, so check first before purchasing your own. Free resources such as insidehighered.com and studentaffairs.com provide news, blogs, and employment opportunities. Each of these resources is also active through social media through Facebook and Twitter. Users who like or follow them are alerted to articles often earlier than the traditional audiences.

Social media has revolutionized professional development opportunities for student affairs. For example, The Student Affairs Collaborative (thesabloggers.org) connects student affairs professionals with the intent of learning with a moderated discussion via Twitter using hashtag #SAchat every Thursday at noon Central Standard Time. This is the new brown-bag workshop. The weekly discussions are archived on the website as well. The popularity of the hashtag has permeated the mainstream and can be found in tweets and posts unrelated to the specific topic. It doubles as an electronic mailing list where professionals are sharing information, asking questions, and supporting each other.

All of these are examples of the types of professional development that could help you achieve your identified competencies. Some of them have a cost associated with them, and others are free, but all of them require time. Making time for professional development is one of the biggest barriers. As you finalize your plan, think about your timeline and try to be both realistic and creative in setting expectations of yourself.

Get Creative

How many times have you complained about having too many resources in your job or office? Probably none. Typically it is the converse. Never enough time. Never enough money. Never enough staff. You could totally, and legitimately, think that way. Or, you could choose to use a different lens and think, I will make time. I will find money. I will ask for assistance and collaboration. Yes, resources are slim, but if you get creative you will often find that you can do more with what you have (time, money, and staff) than you initially thought you could.

Stretching the Dollars (or Cents) for Conferences

Professional development can sometimes be tied to financial resources. Webinars, trainings, institutes, and conferences typically (but not always) come with a price tag. On top of registration fees, there can be travel, lodging, and meal costs. This can be daunting, especially if your institution has little or no funding to devote to staff development, particularly in an individualized sense. One way to get more bang for your buck is to tie yourself to the opportunity; if you are presenting, serving on a committee, or hiring for an open position, it is more likely that your office or institution will view funding you as a developmental and representational investment for the larger whole rather than just for you.

Regardless of who is footing the bill, there are some tips and tricks to minimizing costs for institute and conference attendance. If you are going with a national version, it is smart to choose one that is, if at all possible, on your side of the country. I often pick between ACPA and NASPA based on whichever is being held closest to where I live. Regional or state options are even more cost-effective, and they allow you focus on networking with people who share your locale. Either way, when you are traveling you can scale back the costs by sharing hotel rooms (or not staying at the actual conference hotel or trying a backpacker hostel), packing your own breakfast, hitting up the local grocery store to purchase items to make your own lunch and/or dinner, taking advantage of free conference meals or socials, not purchasing hotel extras (like Wi-Fi), and shelving the coffee habit if you can (the line is too long anyway!). Finally, some experiences offer scholarship opportunities to attend; you can apply to receive funding from the host organization if you meet the established criteria. Putting in a scholarship application does not take that much time, and if you get it, the payoff will be literal and figurative. Also, consider all the free ways you can learn and grow outside of conferences. Think of opportunities to develop on a daily, or monthly, basis instead of waiting for that one time of year when the conference rolls around.

Think Outside the Conference Box

Get out of the mind-set that institutes and conferences are the only options for professional development. Consider webinars: There are free ones! Read seminal works or recently published articles and books: The library has them for free! Keep up with (mostly) free online resources like *The Chronicle of Higher Education, Inside Higher Ed, HuffPost College*, NASPA and ACPA e-mail lists, blogs, #SAchat and other student affairs categories on Twitter, and a laundry list of other options. Set up monthly brown-bag lunch-and-learns for your peer colleagues or your department. Establish an on-campus mentoring program between seasoned professionals and new professionals. Take classes or attend trainings offered by your human resources department. Utilize the opportunity to take, ideally at no cost, classes at your institution (even if you are done with degrees). Schedule recurring phone chats with your mentors and support network. Create a method of cultivating new connections with campus and community partners and colleagues around the country. Reflect. You may be surprised how much you can learn from self-assessment and reflection. Get involved in the community where you live; you can gain many skills from working and volunteering with nonprofit and governmental entities. You get the point, right? Conferences are just one option when it comes to professional development, typically the most costly option. You should look at professional development from a holistic perspective and figure out how to sneak in a little PD every day!

Crafting Your Plan on "Paper"

Thinking and talking about how you plan to continue developing as a professional are necessary first steps. They should also be followed by the second step of actually crafting your plan on "paper." I use quotes around the word *paper* because it does not have to be actual paper; it can be a Word document, Excel list, blog post, or phone to-do list. The key is to put the plan in written words. When we do this, it suggests to us that we are committing to do those things. Consider creating your professional development plan as a career contract for yourself each year. Then share it with someone, or multiple people. Show it to your boss in a one-on-one meeting. Send a copy to the folks in your professional (and maybe personal) support system. Lend it as an example to your supervisees or student staff. Sharing it will encourage you to hold yourself accountable and will open the door for others to hold you accountable too.

The following is the outline for drafting a professional development plan that incorporates all five of the components to a career strategy discussed in this book (so you may have to wait until you finish the book to draft the plan). It is important not only to complete this plan (or something like it) in written form each year but also to continually come back to it to check off the items you have accomplished or attended to and to see what else you have left to explore or do. Now, this should not be an arrangement that makes you feel guilty! If you cannot check everything off the list in the year you planned to, that is okay. Just reflect on why those things did not get done and move those (hopefully) few items to the plan for the following year. Using the five career strategy components, create a professional development plan for yourself in the next year. Include any dates, deadlines, and timelines that you believe would be applicable (see also Appendix C):

- *Skills I want to strengthen and acquire.*
- *Lifelong learning options.* Include topics and areas to explore through reading and research, course work, conferences, meetings, and so on.

- *Committee, presentation, teaching, volunteer, or job experiences to pursue.*
- *Networking or connection tactics to try; people with whom I want to network or connect.*
- *Self-reflection ideas.*

Personal Stories

Professional development is not something that just happens to you. In fact, it is the opposite. Professional development is something that you have to make happen. You have to decide for yourself, with input from others, what knowledge, skills, and experiences you want to seek out and how you can go about acquiring them. You have to assess what resources—financial, time, and human—are available to you on campus, through professional associations, or within your communities. Creating a professional development plan takes intentionality, creativity, dedication, and sometimes a bit of patience.

Next are the stories of four individuals—Allison, Jomita, Jordan, and Jason—whose experiences in higher education range from new professional to associate vice president. They share how they define professional development and how they create opportunities for it in their own careers. Listen to their stories to find out how they continue to grow as student affairs educators each year. Hopefully, their stories will provide insights to how you can craft your own plan for continuous development as a professional.

Allison's Story

Developing a professional development plan ensures we are intentional lifelong learners. Of course, as one of my mentors reiterates, "Have a plan, but be open. Have a plan, but be flexible." Your professional development plan should be a living document that adapts with you on your professional journey. Because most of my student affairs experience is at the same institution, I am committed to continuing to grow and learn as a professional to ensure I am gaining multiple perspectives. Professional development has been instrumental for me. In this story, I share some strategies I have used over the years in planning for professional development.

Staying connected. One of my challenges is staying abreast of the multitude of news, data, and information shared related to higher education and student affairs. However, I am a firm believer that being knowledgeable about current events, trends, and issues is vital to my success as an educator. Ensuring time for student interactions has been one of the best ways for me to stay connected. For the past several years, I have worked directly with our campus's National Association of Student Personnel Administrators (NASPA) Undergraduate Fellows Program and taught an undergraduate student affairs leadership course through the College of Education. I am also passionate about graduate preparation and strive to provide continuous support to our graduate assistants in our higher education program. I greatly enjoy the time I spend with these engaging students. Their excitement is contagious, and it reinvigorates me. Teaching helps hold me accountable to reading current research in preparation for class.

Joining professional associations has benefited me immensely. Professional associations serve, advocate for, and support student affairs through the resources and opportunities they provide. My first student affairs conference was a NASPA Region III Summer Symposium that was only 2 hours driving distance from my home institution. Currently, I serve on the NASPA Region III Board and have continued to enjoy the benefits of being involved at the regional level. My relationships with my NASPA Region III and State of Florida colleagues are some of my most rewarding. We support each other throughout the year outside of NASPA at various regional and state meetings. I consider NASPA my home professional association, and it's where I volunteer more consistently. In addition to NASPA, I am also a member of the American College Personnel Association (ACPA), the Southern Association for College Student Affairs (SACSA), and the Association for the Study of Higher Education (ASHE). The biggest remunerations are the peer-reviewed journals published by these associations, which include the *Journal of Student Affairs Research and Practice* (NASPA), the *Journal of College Student Development* (ACPA), *The College Student Affairs Journal* (SACSA), and *The Review of Higher Education* (ASHE).

Many student affairs divisions, student affairs graduate programs, and campus libraries have subscriptions, so check first before purchasing your own. Free resources such as insidehighered.com and studentaffairs.com provide news, blogs, and employment opportunities. Social media has revolutionized how we manage incoming information and how we share it within our communities. For example, I have been a daily reader of *The Chronicle of Higher Education* since graduate school, but Twitter helps me by identifying key articles to read.

Being proactive. Planning is imperative to setting and achieving goals. I am a firm believer that planning ahead keeps me prepared for future opportunities. As I mentioned earlier, a plan provides structure, but it should be fluid. Whether it was an unexpected promotion or happenstance, my plans have evolved over the years, and a quick learning curve has been essential. The biggest obstacle to this process is time. Being proactive and carving out space in my calendar allows me time to consider my professional future.

A past supervisor of mine encouraged me to conduct self-evaluations annually. The exercise enhanced our conversations. One of the tools I use for self-assessment is the *Professional Competency Areas for Student Affairs Practitioners* (ACPA and NASPA Joint Task Force on Professional Competencies, 2010). This helps me articulate skills gained and provides a framework for new areas of learning. In addition, I track my involvement and role on committees and projects throughout the year. Talking with my supervisor and colleagues to garner feedback on my work provides helpful perspectives. This has worked to my benefit, especially when I need recommendations.

Asking students about their plans always gets me excited. There is so much ahead of them. I get similarly excited when I ask myself those traditional questions, such as, Where do I want to be in 1 year, 5 years, or 10 years? Perusing job postings through *The Chronicle of Higher Education*, higheredjobs.com, or LinkedIn is a quick way to get a pulse of my own marketability. Student affairs is known to inflate titles to compensate for higher salaries. I am always interested to see job descriptions with the same title as mine. I have found this an excellent tool for me to use when building my professional development plans.

Teachable moments. I keep my résumé current, which makes it easier to recognize gaps in my experiences. However, I have also identified learning opportunities by speaking with colleagues or sitting in a meeting and hearing about a topic that sparked my interest. Some of the best opportunities have happened for me because I shared my goals. I truly enjoy hearing people's stories of how they joined the field of higher education. As they shared their journey, I ask them about pitfalls and advice. Never let anyone tell you "thank-yous" are overrated. I try to follow up as soon as possible with my new connections.

Over the years, I have been lucky to have caring supervisors, supportive mentors, and connected sponsors. I am humbled by their confidence in me and am often surprised when they suggest I go for something I did not perceive myself to be "ready for" yet. Recently I attended the NASPA Institute for Aspiring Senior Student Affairs Officers (SSAO) and had the opportunity to meet a group of peers with similar aspirations and interests. We also had the fortune of working with current SSAOs as our faculty for the program. Through the sharing of their experiences, I was able to learn from their successes and missteps. As an example, I came back to my campus and spoke to my supervisor about her process in making difficult decisions. Now when possible I am included in these conversations, which provides me with valuable hands-on experience.

Volunteering. Throughout my career, volunteering has been the fastest way to gain experience and professional development. Supervisors, mentors, and sponsors have volunteered for me in some cases through nominations or recommendations. I also have a close group of friends who serve as my "no" committee to help me process new opportunities. As another one of my mentors says, "Try not to say 'no' if you don't have to. Let someone else say it. Try to find ways to say 'yes.' You may not get another chance." Although it is important to know your limits, being open to new experiences will lead to more opportunities in the future.

Some of my most rewarding experiences came about because I was in the right place at the right time and volunteered. For example, a few years ago I was attending a fall NASPA Region III board meeting in place of a colleague, and the director informed us that the Summer Symposium chair had stepped down. Besides securing the location and date, not much else had been done. The conference was scheduled for the summer in Ponte Vedra, Florida. No one spoke up initially, and then we took a break. I immediately called my supervisor to ask if I could volunteer. He said it was a great opportunity, so I went to the director to express interest. Depending on the project, it may not always be necessary to check in with your supervisor before volunteering. However, if it is a large time commitment and if institutional resources will be needed, you should get your supervisor's approval. The opportunity to lead the Summer Symposium had typically been held for SSAO or director-elect candidates; I was neither. Chairing the Summer Symposium increased my credibility and dependability with my Region III peers and gave me the chance to represent my home institution externally.

Lifelong learning. Professional development is a priority for institutions because it leads to successful recruitment and retention of staff. I believe professional development promotes positive staff morale and prevents us from being complacent. I treasure the time to connect with colleagues, share best practices, and problem solve. I try to be innovative as I plan for professional development by identifying areas that need attention. Professional development that is mission critical helps when it is time to secure travel funding. My personal goal is to have an additional role other than participant at any conference I attend. Some of the ways I achieve this is by volunteering, serving on a committee, or presenting.

Professional development will always be close to my heart. As a lifelong learner, I am committed to my personal and professional growth. I am so thankful to work on a college campus around people who are immersing themselves in learning and becoming active citizens. Keeping up with my professional learning helps me avoid burnout or stagnation. As one of my mentors says, "The cycles of higher education provide us with a natural flow each year. The days, though, are anything but predictable." So true and further supporting why we must continue learning and adapting to prepare for the next group of students.

Jomita's Story

I would not immediately define myself as a creative person. However, I am definitely creative, and always have been, when it comes to thinking about professional development. Creativity is actually a very necessary attribute in designing the ideal professional development portfolio that meets one's personal and professional needs.

My philosophy on professional development is that it should include both personal and professional components and be multifaceted. It is more than simply attending national conferences. It is *so* much more. I believe that strong professional development planning should include mentoring, building professional competency, being involved in your community, and discerning areas you are passionate about, which, for me, is training or development. My professional development plan evolves on an annual basis at minimum (but usually on a monthly basis). I have it on my calendar each month to spend time with my journal (and most recently my Notability app on my iPad) reflecting on the experiences that I have had and updating my plan. To be successful in meeting your professional development goals (and divine purpose for your life), you need to be open and flexible while being intentional, and you *must* write something down. I know that this may not appeal to everyone, and you may not categorize yourself as "that kind of person," but it really is crucial to your success.

To plan means to decide in advance or craft a detailed proposal for how you will achieve something. In essence, it means that you need to write it down. For example, I keep a journal with me at all times so I can jot interesting things down to consider later. I had a goal to get involved in my local community in order to feel more connected and create life-work balance. Therefore, I wrote that goal down and listed all the possible ways I could fulfill it. The list included church, parent-teacher organizations (PTA), social organizations, fitness or athletic associations, and hobby affiliations. Specifically, I got involved in a leadership position in a ministry at my church, ran for a PTA position, purchased a Bikram yoga membership, and researched taking a sewing class. All these opportunities fit into my professional development plan because they help me learn more about myself and exercise my leadership in different areas and have separation from my professional work space.

We are human. Although we have the capacity to remember a lot of information, we also have limited capacity to give all of the information equal space and attention in our mind. In a recent conversation with a mentor, I was reminded that the act of writing is actually exercise for the brain. Writing with a pen or pencil on paper provides multiples types of brain stimulation, thus engaging different parts of the brain. This includes increasing the retention of the information and helping you visualize what you have written! As the old adage goes, "If you see it, then you can be it."

Now that I have made it clear that you need to write down your plan, let's explore what you need to write down. As I said before, I believe that mentoring is an essential element in professional development. It is commonly stated, "It is not what you know but whom you know." I do not totally buy into that idea, but I do believe that relationships are very important in constructing your path and exposing you to different opportunities. It is very valuable to have positive role models and strong networks to assist you in identifying opportunities. I learned about many of the professional development opportunities that are most important to who I am now as an individual and professional through colleagues whom I met who have inspired me and are now mentors to me. For example, I attended a leadership institute for entry-level residence life professionals in my region. While there, I was assigned a mentor who talked with me about the Social Justice Training Institute and LeaderShape. All of which piqued my personal and professional interests. I put them on my list and applied for the opportunities when appropriate. I have held several different roles within each organization and continue to be passionate about their impact on my professional development.

In addition, continually working toward mastery of professional competencies is core to professional development and career advancement. Clearly, you cannot develop professionally without developing personally! For example, I am very passionate about supervision and team development, so I am always looking for ways to grow in this area. I have assisted in the development of workshops within my department, facilitated by senior administrators, to talk about supervision. In addition, I have attended day-long training workshops on supervision, managing and coaching employees, and read several books and articles about team development and professional coaching. Since I started supervising professional staff five years ago, I have always required them to create a professional development plan, which helps me be more accountable as a supervisor and help them reach their personal and professional goals. Furthermore, when I am talking through supervisory situations with my supervisor, human resources, or the like, I use those opportunities to learn from those resources and make professional connections. You can also use mentors to help you identify competencies that are necessary for you to develop based on where you desire to see your career go and to provide a mirror for you to see areas of improvement that you may not be able to identify on your own (and that you do not want your supervisor to have to identify for you!). Some of the competencies that I have articulated for myself include staff development (of course), social justice and multicultural competence, budget management, teaching and training, advising and counseling, and first-year experience.

Community involvement is important in professional development, in my opinion, to help create fulfillment in your life and, potentially, to help you create balance between your personal and your professional needs. For those of us who work outside the home (and actually anyone for that matter), it is really important that we are not only focused on our careers but focused equally on ourselves. For good health and lower stress levels, it is key that we are engaged in activities that fill up our soul. Our soul is what sustains us, and if it is not fed and nourished, then we cannot truly grow. Therefore, identifying opportunities in the community (e.g., church, our children's school, volunteer organizations) for us to contribute to the greater good in a way that makes us feel good about ourselves and our future is crucial to our being able to continue to advance in our professional lives. As shared previously, I had the goal of getting involved in my community as a way to get more connected to my community. This helps me feel even more fulfilled in my professional work space.

Finally, exploring our passion area and identifying ways to develop skills to, ideally, align our career path (current and future positions and job descriptions) are central to professional development seeming not like a chore but rather like a natural part of how we live our lives and approach our work. As I shared earlier, I am passionate about supervision, so I find ways in my current position to do this more and more efficiently. I am also passionate about creating welcoming environments, and there are always opportunities to integrate this into our work. Because I have identified these two areas as things that are important to me, when I am able to focus on and enhance my skills in these areas, I feel energized, and I feel fulfilled. This is what professional development should feel like: energy and fulfillment.

Professional development is a lifelong experience. It also does not always have to cost money. It is a mind-set. It may require financial and human resources to complete your plans. But, if you think big enough and approach each experience with a sense of curiosity and openness to learning, you will be developing professionally even when you are not "trying."

Jordan's Story

Working in student affairs is not something many of us dream we will do. Although there are colleges and universities all over the world, many people I know who work in this field did not dream to be a student affairs practitioner. You simply never see it coming, and you don't know what to expect when you are there. Whether it is how much you loved your undergraduate experience, your passion for education, or your need to be connected to university life, you, like many people, seem to "find" the profession. The question then becomes, How can you create a professional development plan for a world you never knew existed? That challenge often yields some of the greatest realities while working in this field: There are thousands of others who share the same story who are willing to give advice, insight, and wisdom on how to be connected. And that is how professional development began for me.

Once I was admitted to graduate school, professors, students, and university staff told me that I needed to start thinking about my own professional development. As I surveyed the landscape of options available, I had two resources that made a huge impact. One resource was my supervisor in my graduate assistantship. He had worked in student affairs for over 25 years in a variety of institutional types and knew when and where I needed to be connected. The other resource was my graduate cohort. Through our class discussions, socials, and even study time in the library, I learned additional information that would be critical to my professional development plan.

Outside of my official graduate assistant position, my first encounter with professional development arose from networking. I was able to leverage connections made in a professional setting to be involved in opportunities I never thought possible. As a graduate student in a student activities office, I was pushed to attend my first National Association of Campus Activities (NACA) conference in 2006. Once there, I met several people who were heavily involved with NACA, particularly around the need to recruit and retain a diverse young professional group within the association. These individuals had worked closely with the Leadership Fellows program. Its intent was to keep young staff members connected with the association, especially those from underrepresented backgrounds. I was nervous about applying, because the program was relatively new, and I wasn't quite sure how it would help my long-term growth. But, I decided to take a chance and apply to be a fellow. The outcomes from my involvement have been tremendous. As a Leadership Fellow, I was forced to conquer two of my fears: presenting and publishing. I remember my first presentation as if I convened it yesterday. I decided to convene a panel of professionals to speak with current undergraduates and graduate students about what it means to work in student affairs. The feedback I received was honest and helpful and gave me great insight as I continued to conquer my fear of speaking in public. Furthermore, a core component of the fellow program, in addition to presenting at both the regional and the national conferences, is submitting a publication to the NACA *Campus Activities Programming* magazine. Continuing to face these professional fears and perceived weaknesses has been a critical part of my continued professional development.

I used to be someone who feared receiving feedback from others because I feared I might have underperformed on some task. Serving as a Leadership Fellow confirmed that the standards that I set for myself typically exceeded others' standards for me. Consequently, my quest for excellence was really self-determined.

In addition, my involvement within the association has continued to open doors for me. I am no longer afraid to initiate professional conversations with senior-level administrators and understand the value of authentically networking. My passion for student activities and its importance in student retention grew and has led me to be a champion for these programs on other campuses. I also make it a point to stay abreast with research and studies that highlight the role of campus involvement in student retention. All of this happened because I simply decided to take a leap of faith and listen to what my advisor told me.

The real important piece of this story is this: You never know where opportunities will come from. As a senior in college, a graduate student in a master's program, or even a vice president of student affairs, it is always important to be willing to take professional risks and learn about yourself. I knew I had challenges in several areas, and if I want to continually develop as a professional, I need to be willing to face those challenges. Only then am I doing my due diligence to give back to this field, my mentors who have been my champions, and myself. Be willing to take a leap of faith and challenge the areas where you are weak through professional development. It will make a world of difference.

Jason's Story

In March 2010, I was in the midst of the second semester of my graduate program and found myself lucky enough to be attending and presenting at my first national student affairs conference: ACPA Boston. I distinctly remember the nervousness and excitement I felt as I packed my bags the night before and wondered what my experience would be like. What would I learn? Who would I meet? Would my part of the presentation go smoothly? In short, I found that I would learn a tremendous amount and meet many wonderful people, and although I stumbled through most of my part of the presentation, the attendees seemed to have gotten at least something out of it. Three national conferences later, I have made ACPA my professional development home.

Although I have been to only three conferences, I found that I have grown more purposeful with each trip. Going into my first national conference, I remember being extremely overwhelmed by the amount of program sessions offered and ended up going to programs focused on a wide range of topics. In addition, I was very intentional about meeting new people and finding ways to get involved with ACPA, such as running for a directorate position in one of the standing committees. My second year attending the national conference, in 2011, was dedicated mainly to interviewing for jobs; however, I knew I wanted to work in a residential living or international higher education setting and, therefore, attended program sessions on these topics to expand my perspectives of these functional areas. The following year (2012), I had nearly a year of professional experience under my belt, and I realized how easy it was to fail to keep up with current trends and research in higher education. With this in mind, I attended ACPA Louisville with an intentional focus on research-based presentations. In the spring of 2013, I attended my fourth national conference and decided to once again pursue a greater level of involvement in my professional organization by seeking an elected office. In addition, my next professional goal is to gain acceptance into a doctoral program, and I dedicated the 2013 national convention to attending program sessions about applying to doctoral programs, networking with faculty members, and attending sessions that may influence potential dissertation topics.

Conferences are not cheap, and although I have always worked for institutions that are able to support employees' professional development financially, a common complaint that I hear from higher education administrators is how small our professional development budgets can be. However, I have found that with a little creativity and an open mind, one can create many valuable professional development experiences for oneself. For instance, during conference season I have always shared a room with at least one other person and have had friends fit as many as seven people in one room! Also, if the conference is within driving distance, I have found that carpooling can be a fun way to save a few extra dollars. Whether it is jamming to show tunes in the back of a tightly packed vehicle or creatively reciting the contents of the conference program book with your conference roommate(s), methods of saving money through carpooling and sharing rooms can also be a way of building stronger bonds between colleagues, which could be considered professional development in itself.

However, there are also many ways to pursue professional development without attending a conference or spending money. At each institution for which I have worked, one of the first things I investigate is what opportunities are available for me to develop a skill or expand my understanding of the student experience or my chosen career path. These opportunities have included teaching courses in leadership and social justice, serving on departmental committees, or taking part in workshops that teach skills in areas such as graphic design.

In the short time that I have been a student affairs professional, I have found that the most impactful developmental moments I experienced came from making connections with my colleagues and students. The telling of stories can be a truly powerful learning tool, and being open to hearing these stories can give one insight into experiences that no conference session or recent publication can give. At the University of California, Berkeley, I had the privilege of being invited to a "Cal Slam" competition. Cal Slam is a student organization focused on poetry, specifically spoken-word poetry. Over the course of the evening, I listened to 14 student poets each perform two original pieces. Hearing these students reveal their deepest fears and share some of their most closely held secrets, I remember thinking that I have never sat in a class or read a book that illustrated such a raw portrayal of the college student experience. From the students who shared how it felt to be trapped in the closet to students who painted a verbal picture of their depression, I knew that their stories would stay with me throughout my career.

On the other hand, opening myself to the advice of colleagues has been equally effective in my path as a college administrator. I have found some people are receptive only to the advice and experiences of one or two people whom they view as mentors. However, in keeping myself open to hearing about the paths of whatever student affairs practitioner is willing to share, I have been able to make well-informed decisions about my own career and discovered opportunities that may have otherwise not been revealed to me. Reflecting on my career so far, I can see small bits of many colleagues in my professional behaviors, from how I facilitate a staff meeting to how I manage a budget or how I can be a better ally for different student populations.

All in all, developing oneself as a student affairs practitioner is an ever-evolving process. Whether it is attending a conference, teaching a class, or simply listening to others' stories, each person must test the waters and find what works best for him or her.

Chapter Summary

Allison, Jomita, Jordan, and Jason provide great models of how you can seek professional development through a multitude of methods. They also demonstrate that professional development can sometimes be achieved through personal development and involvement outside of higher education. Professional development is about self-growth, and it is your responsibility to determine what you want to learn, how you can learn it, and who you need to connect with to make it happen. It is also about getting creative and thinking holistically about the options available in order to achieve development on a daily, rather than yearly, basis. This chapter gives you some ideas about how you can begin to craft a professional development plan. The key here is this: Do not just think about it, talk about it, or write about it. Be about it!

Note

1. The majority of this section was written by Dr. Allison Crume, associate vice president of student affairs at Florida State University.

NETWORKING OR
CONNECTING

With contributions by Robert "Bobby" Borgmann,
Lindsey Katherine Dippold, Sara Jones,
Claudia Mercado, and Raja Bhattar

Relationships take time, getting to know folks requires patience,
and people are generally cautious—if not fearful—of
"Johnny come lately" that is asking, rather than giving.

—Jeremiah Owyang

I define connection as the energy that exists between people when they feel seen,
heard, and valued; when they can give and receive without judgment;
and when they derive sustenance and strength from the relationship.

—Brené Brown

The currency of real networking is not greed but generosity.

—Keith Ferrazzi

Do You!

Student affairs, like many fields, is centered on relationships. You should not, and cannot, operate in a silo. Well, you could try. But, it would probably not result in an optimal situation for you or anyone else. So, hear this: Building relationships is fundamental. It is step one. It is the very first thing you should focus on when entering the field and each time you begin a new job or role. You will need to cultivate relationships with some, or all, of the following groups: supervisors, colleagues, supervisees, students, parents, alumni, boards, vendors, educational nonprofit agencies, professional organizations, and so on. This goes for everyone, no matter if you call yourself extroverted

106

or introverted! You must, I repeat, you must learn how to build, maintain, strengthen, and restore relationships. And doing that is a personal process. People go about relationships in their own way, which is fine because there is not one "right" way to do it.

I tend to build relationships on my campus by getting to know people in a one-on-one manner. Each time I embark upon a new job, I spend a significant amount of time (some would say too much time) setting up one-on-one meetings with anyone on campus with whom our office currently partners and anyone with whom we may partner in the future. I use the meetings to learn about people—who are they, where are they from, what do they care about, what makes them tick—and about the office where they work—what is the mission, whom do they see as their population, what are their signature programs, how do they see our areas teaming up. This time is important because it is the catalyst I can use to cultivate a relationship with that individual and, subsequently, with his or her office. Then, I follow up. That's the key! I do not do a "one and done." Rather, I write an e-mail thanking people for their time. I provide them with any information they may have requested. I begin working on any ideas or projects that we mentioned in the meeting. I maintain the relationship and look for ways to strengthen it.

Similarly, at professional conferences and other professional development opportunities (e.g., facilitating programs for national organizations), I look for people with whom I want to connect on a one-on-one basis. Actually, to keep it real, sometimes I choose those individuals, and other times they choose me. But, the structure is still the same: Find some time when you can have a genuine, one-on-one discussion with the person, even if it is just for 5 or 10 minutes, and discuss who you are, what matters to you, and how you can work together on something—anything! Then, follow up. That process is precisely how some of the personal stories ended up in this book. I went somewhere, met someone, kept in contact, and then asked the person if he or she was interested in being part of this project.

When you cannot find the few minutes for a solo conversation or can find someone only in a passing moment, then grab her or his business card. Write a few things on the back of it: (a) a way to remember the person whether it is what she or he was wearing or whom she or he was walking with, (b) when and where you met her or him, and (c) something you have in common with her or him or something you want to learn more about. Then, follow up! Are you starting to see the pattern?

Another step I take in my relationship-building process is to bring people with me. Not literally. But, as I move around to different jobs in different locations, I make sure to sustain the relationships I have established by keeping up with people. I check in via e-mail, I update myself on others' moves through Facebook, and I follow certain people on Twitter. I even call people to catch up every so often—that's right, I actually dial numbers on the phone. I use every communication means I can think of to both maintain and strengthen the relationships I have put time and effort into and that matter to me.

Finally, I reflect and recognize when a relationship needs to be restored. Whether communication lapsed because of me or the other person, whether time just "got away" from us, or whether we had some kind of issue, when I decide that a relationship needs some work, I will (try really hard to) put in the work from my end. Sometimes that is as easy as one e-mail. Other times, it may take years of attempting to connect, having (possibly tough) conversations, and determining if the relationship can be rebuilt.

Let me be clear, though. Although my process works for me, it will not work for everyone. I know that. You know that. It suits me because I have a solid memory for faces, and I have no qualms with approaching anyone and saying, "I know I know you but cannot recall from where" or "I see you went to [insert school]! I had [insert experience] there." I am also very open to having people do the same to and with me. If you have not already guessed, I identify as an extrovert. I can do large groups pretty easily, but what may surprise you is that I do prefer to get to know people in an individual, in-depth way. I believe it gives me a more genuine understanding of the person and encourages continuance of the connection. The point is this: You will need to discover what relationship-building process works for you.

Choose the Term You Like

The first aspect of determining how you can best build relationships is using the terminology that speaks (no pun intended) to you. For as long as I can remember, I have been preached to about the importance of networking. Network, network, network! But, networking has a somewhat tarnished reputation. Some tend to associate it with schmoozing and, thus, with being fake or a kiss-ass (pardon the curse word). Or, they think of it as a task that only extroverts can accomplish. Conversely, others adore it. They read every book or news article ever written on networking tactics and try all of them in one sitting.

In short, the term *networking* does not conjure up a pleasant experience for everyone. If that is true for you, steer clear of thinking of this process as networking. Instead, consider using the term *connecting*. Practice it as relationship building or relating to others. Deem it making friends. Take into account that it is learning about others' experience, time, and talents and, then, sharing your own. Use whatever term or phrase encourages you to get to know people with whom you share your career field.

Know Your Style and Find Your Kind of Context

Once you have settled on a term that aligns with how you operate, you need to explore your style and context of cultivating relationships. I described my style for you, and the personal stories at the end of this chapter shed light on some other people's styles, but I cannot tell you what your style looks like. That is for you to discover and nurture. You will have to learn if you prefer seeking relationships or waiting for others to initiate them. You will have to try various methods of meeting people through professional development. You will have to determine how you best communicate with others and create collaborative projects. It will be a trial-and-error process, and that is okay.

Your style will likely correspond with the type of context in which you prefer to meet people and build relationships. One-on-one may work better for you. If so, you should seek out one-on-one meetings in your job and smaller institute-type professional development opportunities. On the other hand, if you believe that more is merrier, then you may look to create larger group contexts by organizing colleague lunch hours and seeking out national conferences for professional development. It is also important to recognize that you can influence the context of situations. For example, if you prefer solo conversations with another individual but you tend to find yourself at large conferences, work ahead of time (or on-site) to set up one-on-one meetings with colleagues over meals and during breaks. Or, if you find yourself at a small institute, organize a meal or night out that includes everyone there. The point is that you can create the context you feel most comfortable in if you do a tiny bit of coordination.

Go in All Directions

A final aspect of relationship building to consider is with whom you plan to develop connections. It may be tempting to focus only on people who are your senior because those are typically the people you feel have "made it" (whatever that means!). Yes, you can learn a lot from these types of individuals. And, by all means, you should get to know some folks who have the experience and wisdom that you hope to gain. However, I think it is beneficial to cultivate relationships all over the organizational chart and experience continuum.

Let me start with your actual job. It is vital to get to know not only your supervisors and colleagues but also your supervisees, any students or alumni with whom your office interacts frequently, and vendors from whom you will purchase goods or services. And, try not to stop there either. What about meeting faculty? Administrators within the business functions of the institution? And, in my opinion, the people who really run things: the administrative assistants and custodial staff? I always make a point to get to know the custodial and cashier staff in the student centers where I have worked, maybe because my parents have those types of jobs, but mostly because service staff are people just like me, and all of us together create the campus community. If you get to know only the people "above" (for lack of a better word) you, you will be missing out on a large crop of folks with whom you can build relationships to make everyone's day job easier and more fulfilling.

A similar mind-set should be taken into professional development opportunities. Try to refrain from focusing on just the "important" or "high-profile" names at the event. Go on and attempt to meet those people, fine, but please do not be "too good" to meet new professionals, graduate students, or undergraduates who are exploring the field as a possible career choice. Every individual has something to contribute! Personally, I have learned just as much from the younger professionals with whom I have connected as I have from the seasoned professionals. I tend to think of my network as fivefold: (a) the people who have been there longer and can provide historical context and insight from that angle (seasoned professionals); (b) the people who share my station in the field and can relate to my current situation (peers); (c) the people who generally have the best frontline pulse on the latest literature and student culture (younger professionals, graduate students, and undergraduates); (d) the people who know the logistical processes, manage daily functions, and keep the place operational (administrative and custodial staff); and (e) the people who provide external perspectives and resources (national organizations and community members and organizations). I need to cultivate all five types of relationships in order to garner a holistic picture of the student affairs field and create an understanding of the past, present, and future of higher education.

Finally, you should spend some of your time focusing on relationships outside of higher education. Meet people in your community. Talk to people on planes. E-mail that person who your friend from back home suggested you get to know. You never know who will be a solid connection for you professionally, personally, or both.

Politics

So far I have discussed relationship building without mentioning constraints. If only the world, or even just higher education, were that simple. Just to be clear—it's not. When it comes to building relationships, you must give significant consideration to politics. Yes, politics. Now, I am not talking about your political affiliation or personal ideology. I am referring to what is called "office politics," although it generally extends outside of your work space to the overall institution and the field at large.

Please do not stop reading here because you "don't play politics." Although that may be your ideal, you will—at the least—have to learn how to navigate politics. If you do not, it could be detrimental to you or to the office or department in which you work. If it helps, think of navigating politics like playing chess. You need to know who the players are, when they may interact with one another, and how they work together to protect something—the queen in the case of chess; programs, budget, reputation, your job, and other similar aspects in the case of higher education. Much like playing chess, learning how to navigate the process may take longer than you would like and may involve moving two steps forward and three steps back.

Departmental

Within each office and/or department, there will be an agenda set by someone. Maybe it will be directly linked to the divisional or institutional strategic plan, maybe it will be set by the department head or director, maybe the entire team will contribute to creating it, or likely it will be a combination of all three. Regardless, an agenda exists, and it is important for you to know what it is and how your area contributes to meeting it. If your area does not focus on the agenda, then it is not useful to the overall office or department, and it will not be given much time or attention by "the powers that be." Make sure people in your unit know what you are doing, why you are doing it, and how it will make the office or department look good in front of the division.

Divisional

The next phase of politics is on the divisional level. For most of you reading this book, that will be either the Division of Student Affairs or Division of Student Life or a combined Division of Academic and Student Life (see Chapter 1 for more information on how divisions are set up). The goal is to make sure that the senior student affairs officers (the assistant and associate vice presidents or chancellors: AVPs or AVCs) and the chief student affairs officer (the vice president or chancellor: VP or VC) see your office or department not only as essential to the division but also as a major provider of solid student learning experiences. Keep your supervisor abreast of anything you have going on so he or she can answer any questions the AVP (or AVC) and VP (or VC) may ask. Tie in your programs and services to the divisional goals and strategic plan. Show through assessment what students are gaining from their experiences with your area. Know where you are spending your money, and have sound reasons for using it in that manner. In short, be solid enough to be the functional area that divisional leaders want to showcase to the entire institution.

In addition, learn who the key people are across the division. Do you have a good contact in each office or department? If not, get to building those relationships! Do you know who has your back and who does not? If not, become aware. Whether or not you like it, you will have both allies and adversaries. Better to know the distinction than not know.

Note that there is a caveat to politics as you begin to build relationships outside of your department and across the division: It is essential that you maintain an awareness of hierarchies and "chains of command." You do not have to like this. You do have to recognize that it exists and how it may impact you if you do not follow rank protocol. For example, your office or department director should probably know information before you share it with the assistant vice president (i.e., the director's boss). If you "jump rank," it may leave the director in a very awkward position of having to answer questions about something on which she or he was not informed and can lead to a perception that the director does not have a pulse on her or his area. Neither of these scenarios would result in a positive outcome for you either. So, be proactive. Run ideas by your supervisor. Give people a heads-up when you plan to have a significant meeting. Copy appropriate folks on your e-mails. Make sure that you are not leaving anyone "up the chain" unprepared or blindsided. It will benefit everyone. I promise.

Institutional

Similar to the divisional politics, there are overall institutional politics to understand. It gets a bit muddier here because this political sphere often pits offices and divisions against one another for scarce financial, time, and human resources, as well as attention from the overall university administration (chancellor or president and board). Again, it is important to develop a platform that highlights the value of your functional area and also make the overall institution look good. It is a delicate balance.

Another aspect of institutional politics is finding partners across divisions with whom you can collaborate. Nothing makes a chancellor or president more pleased than examples of how student affairs is partnering with academic, alumni, or business affairs to get a task accomplished. Again, creating a network of colleagues throughout the entire institution—up and down the organizational chart—is a crucial factor. Build relationships. Know who are your "go-to" people or offices. Find ways to share costs around common goals. Share the credit (but do keep some of it for your area and you). Make the overall institution see your functional area and you as both stable and pioneering.

The same caveat discussed in the previous divisional section also applies to the institutional context: Respect rank. This is probably even more important on the institutional level because the division wants to send a consistent, uni-fied message out across campus and focus on its strategic priorities. For exam-ple, if you want to seek funding for a program through private donations by partnering with university advancement and development, you should first ask your supervisor if that is permitted and/or encouraged. If it is, then you should make sure that you, or your supervisor, clear the request with all the necessary people to ensure that your request is not competing with other divi-sional appeals and that you have approval to reach out to university advance-ment and development to cultivate a relationship. And, whatever you do, call people by their title (Dr., Chancellor, etc.) unless they tell you not to!

Now, this practice of hailing to the hierarchy can be complex, not only because it may seem stifling but also because you may run into the rare case where someone in the rank(s) above you is making a decision that is actually unethical, illegal, or in direct contrast to your values. This is the point where you would have to make some tough decisions on whether the transgression is worth "breaking rank." It may also come to the juncture where you have to make a call about whether staying at the job is right for you or if you should seek new opportunities. And, the "black-and-white" scenarios of this—like stealing funds or providing substances to minors—is not where things get tricky. Rather, it is the "gray areas"—such as subtle discrimination during hiring practices or the elusion of policy requirements—that create complex situations where you may not have proof or are reluctant to report the poten-tial transgression. Regardless of the scenario, there is always anxiety about repercussions of revealing damaging decisions, and rightfully so. How you choose to handle it will be framed, in large part, by your campus's protocol (through human resources and your division), the severity of the situation, and your personal "line(s) in the sand."

With External Partners

You will also have to understand the contextual situation with external part-ners in the surrounding community and vendors with whom your office contracts programs or services. Your office or department may heavily inter-act with nonprofit agencies, businesses, or national or international organiza-tions. It is important to learn who are the best contacts for those partnerships, understand where those relationships stand when you enter the situation, and create plans for how to maintain and strengthen those partnerships.

In the Field

Outside of your workplace and community, you will face politics in the over-all field of student affairs. The difference in this case is that the politics are more personal than job related. There are certain graduate programs and institutions that have better networks and look out for "their own" more than others. There are particular ways to write conference session proposals that tend to increase the probability of acceptance. There are specific experiences that you have or do not have that make you part of the "in group" or "out group." There are colleagues and mentors who will have you as a sidekick and introduce you to hordes of people and others who will leave you to your own devices. It is a complex system.

One solid piece of advice regarding politics within the overall field is this: Be extremely careful of what you say, to whom you say it, and where you have conversations. This was preached to me during my first round of graduate school, and it was a wise caution. I also reinforced the lesson firsthand at a national conference. I was (thankfully!) praising a book I had read and the session I had just attended by its author and suggesting to one of my faculty members that she should use it in an upcoming class. After I was done with my soliloquy, I felt a tap on my shoulder. I turned around to face the author of the book! She told me she was glad I enjoyed her work and thanked me for lobbying for it to become a course text. I was in shock. Fortunately, I had been saying something positive. But, what if the case were the opposite?! I would have created a negative situation for others and myself and possibly tarnished my name with both a respected author and my faculty member. So, be wary of elevators, hotel restaurants and bars, and any professional development session, among other arenas. You want to build bridges, not burn them.

The other adage I was taught about political savvy is to choose your battles wisely. This is another solid morsel of wisdom, although it is not as easy to choose as you might initially think. Picking battles is a multipart activity. It requires that you know yourself and your line(s) in the sand well, that you fully grasp what the protected interests and programs are at the institution (particularly the ones that impact your area) or within the field, and that you determine which battles are worth gambling your, and your office's or institution's, reputation on. And please note: Throughout your career, there will (and I mean *will*) be points where you pick the wrong battle. Just try to choose wisely more often than not.

Personal Stories

Building relationships and navigating politics take time and effort, more so for some of us than others. You have to learn with whom, how, and where you feel the most sincere about cultivating connections. You have to decide how (not if!) you will participate in the varying levels of politics within student affairs. And know this: None of that is simple or easy. But you can, and will, do it!

The following are the stories of five individuals—Bobby, Lindsey, Sara, Claudia, and Raja—who participate in the field of higher education. They share how they utilize relationships and navigate politics in their careers and personal lives. Listen to their stories to find how they incorporate networking and connecting tactics to create support systems, find new opportunities, and deal with the complexities of navigating their offices, institutions, and the field at large. Hopefully, their stories will provide insights to how you can assemble your own troupe of mentors, colleagues, and acquaintances.

Bobby's Story

One of the most important aspects of student affairs and higher education is how you are able to connect with others. Networking and creating relationships with those in the profession are critical to one's success. I was lucky to cultivate many great relationships with individuals along my journey who have helped prepare me for where I am today.

Graduate school was really where I was able to build a strong foundation for my professional network. I never realized how your classmates and the graduates from your program could really serve as a strong support system for you. My program gave me many great friends and colleagues who have provided me with great feedback, insight, and knowledge that I have taken with me throughout my career.

I never really understood the value of networking until I started applying for summer internships during my first year of graduate school. I ended up landing an internship with the University of Tennessee–Knoxville, where a graduate of my program was an assistant director. She knew me from my time as a student leader and served as one of my advisors while she was a graduate student herself. This person was able to give me insight and mentorship in areas that I was actively seeking. Through my graduate program, I was able to meet so many people from so many different places, and I was able to learn from them and their experiences. Each person brought something new to the conversation. From their experiences as resident assistants to their ideas about how law in higher education could be applied to specific court cases, we were able to bounce experiences off one another to help us become better professionals. I also learned that your classmates will be great resources once you start your career. You never know where you will end up and who will be working alongside you. I realized that when you have people on the employer's side of the conversation, your network comes in handy. While I was job searching in my last semester of graduate school, several alumni from my program put me in contact with several different institutions because of their professional networks, helping me land interviews with a few universities in Florida and Texas. Alumni support through graduate programs always plays a large role in the job search.

As a graduate student, you really get hands-on experience as a full-time professional through internships. Luckily for me, I was not the only intern that summer at UT–Knoxville. David Stout from the University of South Carolina was with me for an experience of a lifetime. We shared information about our programs, talked about what we could do to assist each other and our orientation leaders, and just kept each other going when the long days came around. Once our internship ended, we stayed great friends, constantly giving each other updates on the things that are going on in our lives and careers. We even send job postings to one another from our institutions because we know working together again could be in our future. At conferences, we are able to introduce each other to our own colleagues and further expand our contacts and networks.

That summer also provided me a great friendship that has directly affected me in my functional area. I work with my institution's programming board and homecoming, overseeing most of the student-run programming at the university. When I began working in my new role, I attended the National Association for Campus Activities (NACA) southern conference. I was brand-new to the area of programming and did not know much of what was going on. I was lucky to see a familiar face, one whom I met while she was a graduate student at UT–Knoxville: Tyger Glauser. Tyger now works at Coastal Carolina University and oversees its programming board. When we first saw one another at the conference, she was willing to inform me of everything she possibly knew about the association and introduced me to other staff members who sat on the regional conference planning committee. This was valuable for me, as it helped me expand my network in the field and gave me additional resources. She and I quickly talked about doing a presentation together for the following year's conference, and our presentation ended up being accepted and well attended. This helped me understand the importance of branching out from my institution and making connections with other professional staff members from different institutions in the region. It also taught me the importance of presenting at conferences. It not only gives you the chance to meet new individuals from around the country but also assists in promoting your skills as a presenter and at your institution.

My new understanding of this functional area, along with my newly formed resources, helped me also do something that I am passionate about: writing. Because I love writing so much, I knew I wanted to start having my work published, so I turned to the NACA *Campus Activities Programming* magazine. It was here that I was able to submit an article on marketing strategies and tips for university programming boards. I was able to create a great working relationship with the editor and will continue to submit articles whenever I can. This was all made possible because of the connections and resources I made through NACA.

Because of my personal experiences, I always recommend volunteering in national organizations. Although NACA is one association that I have volunteered with, another one that has challenged me more than any other is the LeaderShape Institute. I have the privilege to assist in the programming for the South Florida LeaderShape Institute, which is a consortium inclusive of seven universities in South Florida. Through this, I have been able to meet administrators from various institutions who all share a common vision: seeing students succeed on our campuses and beyond. This experience helped me gain new colleagues and allies at new institutions across the state. It was through my LeaderShape experience that one of the lead facilitators approached me with an opportunity to contribute to a book—the one you are reading right now. The feedback that I have received, along with the genuine care and interest of those involved with the LeaderShape Institute, has helped me grow exponentially as a professional. I have gained mentors, friends, and colleagues whom I can contact if ever I have a question or concern.

The easiest way to meet new people in this profession is to branch out, shake hands, and put yourself out there. If not for the experiences that I have had thus far, my career path might look very different than it does today.

Lindsey's Story

"It's all about *who* you know, not *what* you know." "Up to 70% of first jobs are found through networking." How many times have you asked people how they found their way into their career, and the answer was a seemingly random tale of being in the right place at the right time or connecting with a person who led them there? These clichés and tales are common because of the simple fact that life is about connecting. Well, it involves more than that, of course, but relationships add meaning to life. Hence, cultivating relationships, both personal and work related, is something that I have valued since the beginning of my career. I have been intentional about connecting with others in my field, and the networking aspect has followed.

As I reflect on how I have used networking and connections in my own career, a few patterns of my approach emerge.

More is more. My implicit curiosity of how things work led me to cross traditional boundaries. I wanted to know how other student affairs offices worked on campus. I wanted to know why academic affairs offices seemed to operate so differently. I wanted to learn from the mistakes and share in the novel ideas from other, similar institutions. My thirst for knowledge was simple and collaborative: The more people I connect with, the more I will learn about their story, and the more I will be able to apply their related concepts to my own life and work. I did this any way I could, but rather than simply asking questions, I tried to take a more active approach. I took on internships or short projects in other offices as part of my doctoral course work. I shadowed our leaders. I volunteered for campus-wide committees and state and regional associations. But you can't say "yes" to everyone. I was selective with what I chose to participate in and tried to find the most mean-ingful projects, relevant to my interests, because we all know there is never enough time for it all! Before agreeing to become involved, I always asked myself what the potential benefits were for those involved (What can I give them?), what benefits were likely for me (What will I take away?), and what was the risk of the time commitment (What might I miss out on because of this commitment?). It seems simple enough, and this helped me become more invested in all of the experiences, from simple committee meetings to full conference planning. It also helped me justify saying "no" to opportuni-ties that did not fit my goals.

Set targets. The importance and benefit of connecting are clear. But how do we find people to connect with? I recommend a multitiered approach. Yes, I actually make notes and diagrams about which offices, institutions, and administrators I hope to learn more about and why. Identifying potential partners on your own campus is a good starting place. Then I became heavily involved in the state organization within my field, working up to identifying regional contacts at comparable institutions.

Personal style. It is vital that you evaluate your own personal style. I am *not* a "woo-er." I'm only slightly more extroverted than I am introverted according to Myers-Briggs, and the idea of being in a room mingling with 50 strangers can be invigorating or exhausting depending on my mood and the group. Thus, I have different techniques to help when my desire to make connections is fading. My favorite is to ask people a lot of questions about themselves. This will ensure there is no awkward silence, and people usually find it very easy to talk about themselves. It is a lazy form of networking, but it will get you warmed up. If at all possible, I try to coerce someone I already know into making the rounds with me. I have some interesting friends and colleagues, which helps get the conversations going.

There are other ways I found to connect beyond participating in the traditional networking event. When possible, I volunteer to help work on some aspect of the event. Doing this will give you a specific task to focus on, and people will inherently think you are important when donning a fancy name tag. It allows you time to get to know the group better. If you are working a registration table, you'll put faces with names and meet everyone immediately, so you can find them later. This is useful not only at networking events but also at conferences, workshops, and even campus meetings. Another tactic is volunteering for leadership positions within organizations. Creating the monthly newsletter, editing the website, coordinating membership renewal, and planning conferences are all jobs I did within my state organization, and it helped me to learn a great deal about what the organization was about and who was a part of it.

Give to get or just give to give. The problem with networking is that it is easy to wonder, "What can this person do for me?" but the beauty of connecting is that it is so much more rewarding when you think about what you have to give. Know your strengths and think of how you can help your connections. Strengths of mine are organizing and executing. I cannot come up with the novel ideas, but if you do, I can make them happen. Committees love and need that person. What you have to give doesn't have to be service. It can be as simple as reading an article, job posting, and so on and thinking "Who might benefit from this information?" and passing it along or sending thoughtful messages during a busy season or holiday.

Networking isn't everything. Some of my positions came from meeting the right people and being in the right place. However, some of my positions didn't. I applied just like everyone else as an "outsider." I made sure my résumé was flawless and contained quality content, wrote a convincing cover letter, and prepared a great deal for the interview. This is just a reminder that networking and making connections should be only one piece of your career strategy.

As I find myself in a new city, in a new part of the country, beginning again and reflecting on my career path, I have one piece of advice I will offer in closing. Had I, in my wildest imagination, thought I would end up here, I would have been broader in my networking and connections. I put effort into building a strong network of colleagues and friends in Florida, where I spent several years and thought I would stay. You may think you know where your career path or personal life is directed, but you never really know for sure! Don't discount opportunities that you may enjoy because you can't see the immediate value, and keep an open mind when connecting with professionals from areas outside of your region or expertise.

Sara's Story

The value of building and cultivating personal relationships and connecting people to each other and organizations is what I do and what I love, and I am blessed to do it within the environment of higher education. Listening to and observing others have often helped point me in the professional direction to go (or not go), given me some helpful hints in figuring things out, and provided me with people with whom I trust to have the conversations.

I have been extremely lucky, blessed, and fortunate to create amazing relationships throughout my professional journey. I attended a midsize, regional public institution for my undergraduate degree. It was a largely commuter campus, though the administration was making strides to significantly engage the on-campus population. Literally from my first semester, thanks to a great resident assistant and a friend I knew through high school involvement, I became active in many aspects of cocurricular college life.

After I changed majors three times and decided that as an organizational communication major I would become an event planner, a mentor said, "I can see you going in to higher education student affairs." My response was, "Maybe someday, but I want a 'real' job first." Fast-forward past an internship in a university advancement office, graduation, and a job search. While working full-time for a nonprofit association, I started missing the energy of a college campus. So I reached out to the community I had built at my undergraduate institution, signed up for the GRE, and started applying to graduate programs in higher education.

Then I ended up someplace I said I would never attend, because people I trusted assured me it was a really good place. As soon as I met the faculty in the program, staff and administrators from student affairs, and current students, I knew it was a good fit for me. Throughout my career, "fit"—that internal feeling I've gotten from a place—and conversations with mentors have helped me figure out if I am going to accept an offered position and be okay when the answer is no.

My acceptance into the higher education master's program and a graduate assistantship working with the student affairs development officer provided me with opportunities to work with an amazing group of higher education professionals, including student affairs and university development, alumni, and current students. Projects for my assistantship and other internships required the ability to work with each of the offices in the division of student affairs, multiple areas across campus, and the local community. I connected with people across all areas with whom I still remain in contact. Simply having regular access to our vice president for student affairs (and seeing the university president come into the office) and her administrative staff and directors was beyond beneficial when it came to observing campus politics. Being able to talk about those observations with my supervisor and other senior staff members taught me lessons I continually reflect on.

Those graduate school experiences also helped me process various environments as I have moved from position to position throughout my career. I realized early on that learning the politics and institutional quirks of an environment is key before setting out an agenda for change (yes, within the first few months of a new job, I told a supervisor my long-term plan for my position and how I imagined significant organizational restructuring). Although this may have shown some initiative, it also disregarded the politics, organizational climate for change, and any opinions and reactions my supervisor may have had to my observations.

I have always put a lot of value in my face-to-face relationships and maintaining them through calls, e-mails, and handwritten notes. And, I place even more value on what I can learn from those around me. When I interviewed for my position at Penn State's Alumni Association, I told the students I met with that they would have to teach me what it meant to be a Penn Stater if I was offered and accepted the position. I know I am capable of succeeding in many jobs, but I like being all in—going feet first into a new position, meeting the constituents, figuring out the challenges, and making sure that people buy in to me serving in the position.

In the past few years, I have added additional abilities to my relationship-building skill set. A student I worked with for a while tried to convince me of the value of Twitter. I argued that 140 characters was not enough space to build a connection or truly share information. Now, I've connected and reconnected with colleagues across the country. I have used Twitter to help me find job opportunities and engage in a new community when I knew I was moving. And, Twitter serves as a level playing field for hierarchical organizations; I have tweeted with vice presidents and prospective students, and all of them have an equal voice in the "Twitterverse." I have become more mindful about developing my social presence and taking advantage of the opportunities to engage with new people and follow conference back channels and share information that could be helpful to others. I find these things to be incredibly valuable.

You never know when the connections from a former colleague will support you in a future endeavor. Thanks to a former supervisor engaging with a person at my new institution, I was invited to be a part of a divisional task force that I did not even know existed in an area I am passionate about (but not currently working in). Other days, it is just reassuring to attend a conference and see the smiling faces of people who used to work down the hall.

So get to know people. Learn about their perspective, do great work, and never say never. You do not know when you will be able to share a great idea or have the opportunity to help build a dream team. And when the time comes, it is always great to have a deep bench a phone call, e-mail, or tweet away.

Claudia's Story

Growing up Mexican, I am sure I was supposed to remain a stereotypical quiet girl who gets lost in the shadows. I think my family has some chromosome problem, because all the women in my family are talkers. We love to meet new people and learn from our newfound friendships. However, it is not simply about making more new friends; we women really like to make strong connections. You never know when your new friend will need a ride to the airport or when you will need your friend to be by your side during tragedy. I see this trait in my older sister, my mom, and my grandmother. Although we are not the typical Mexican women, this skill has allowed all of us to move forward through life in our own ways.

My most meaningful connections have happened when I was a volunteer in the community. While I was employed at the University of Kansas, I was asked by a student to advise a new multicultural sorority. It was a really small chapter, and I liked the fact that I could help the women, being a Greek member of a small sorority myself. I developed a strong relationship with the women and later learned that one member was volunteering at Big Brothers Big Sisters, and I decided to mentor a seventh grader. After a short while of mentoring and attending Big Brothers Big Sisters events, I was asked to serve on the board of directors at the local level. My one-on-one connection with a student and willingness to help her with a cause that was mutually important to us led me to become one of Big Brothers Big Sisters' youngest board members. The board members saw me as a conduit to future university employee volunteers, and that is exactly what I gave them.

After I moved to Chicago, I began to utilize the many services available for the LGBTQ community. After doing some research, my partner and I joined Dignity Chicago, a Catholic LGBTQ organization. I know, it's a paradox for some, but for us we found a home with other people who could practice their faith in a welcoming and affirming environment. We jumped in and began helping with all events and connecting with other members in small settings. After earning the member of the year award, we were asked to serve on the board of directors on a shared position. Through the years, we remained engaged and helped in as many events as possible.

The connection with Dignity Chicago and the one-on-one connection my partner made with a classmate from law school led us to another meaningful volunteer opportunity. We were asked to serve on a historic state lawsuit for same-sex marriage in Illinois, representing LGBTQ families. Now we were one of 16 couples to represent the entire state, and our new role as the young, long-term, lesbian, Hispanic family with two kids made us an ideal candidate for the lawsuit. We often hear, "We saw you on the news the other night," and not through vanity I have to ask, "Really? What was I wearing?" I ask this question not because I have a bad memory but because my family has been videotaped and photographed extensively over the past couple of years. I would not have imagined the small connections with individuals would have led us to be a part of this significant battle.

I would say these three examples of connections have two main themes in common. One, my connection style is more one on one and in small group settings. I am not big on distributing business cards to the masses, because the ones I have collected remain in the bottom of some conference bag. One-on-one and small group networking events work well for me because of the depth of connection I need. This is not everyone's style, but I have learned that in the larger group, I do become that stereotypical little Mexican girl who sits quietly. However, if that large room is composed of tables and if I am given a moment to connect with the person next to me, we might become lifelong friends. You have to find the space that works best for you in which you find your most authentic self coming to life. That space will always produce great results both personally and professionally.

Two, my connections have had a strong sense of meaningfulness for me. This has always been important to me, because the more meaningful the connection, the more likely I am to volunteer and become a part of the organization and, in addition, the more likely I become to find mentors, bring in new faith members, or spend hours speaking to reporters and smiling for the Associated Press photographer. In leadership terms, I would define myself as a servant leader. Once you determine what passions or causes drive you to be the best contributor, you will find countless opportunities to step into leadership roles and expand your network.

Although none of the examples I provided are related directly to my job or my professional organizations, these connections have helped me professionally indirectly in three ways. First, my volunteer experiences have helped me strike a balanced work-life ratio, which in higher education and student affairs can be rather challenging. I realize that 40 hours per week in higher education is not a long enough workweek, but when I have other responsibilities, 40-ish hours of work will have to suffice. Second, my connections have helped me find mentors who could help me cope with the strenuous challenges of work. I must release my challenges verbally in order to remain a competent employee and supportive supervisor. My mentors are significant in helping me see more clearly and challenging me to become a better version of myself. Finally, these connections have helped me connect to a world off a university campus in which I have remained more than half my life now and provide me with a "refresh" opportunity so I can come back to campus and remain excited about the work I do.

Whether you connect with professional organizations, nonprofits, or social justice agencies, my advice is to connect well. Give meaning to the relationships you develop, and have a purpose to what you do. You never know what can happen. I guess I am proud of my cultural chromosome problem, and I am proud to be in the company of strong women in my family.

Without it, I wouldn't have made so many connections so soon. Without it, I wouldn't have made the connection that led me to write this story.

Raja's Story

Who knew learning a card game could guide me to a variety of professional networks and employment opportunities?

In 2010, I quit a job I loved because I was ready for a change and had the opportunity to travel with Semester at Sea, a study abroad program for college students traveling to several countries. In addition to traditional students, there were some lifelong learners on the voyage. A family of 15 called the Bender family happened to be on the voyage. The patriarch was Dave, a humble person who had been financially very successful because of a book series he developed to support critical thinking among high school students during his years as a teacher. I knew nothing else about him or the rest of the Benders until I grew tired of seeing them all playing a strange card game in the dining hall for hours after each meal. Wanting to see what this was about, I asked to join in and soon became a convert and an "honorary Bender," arranging my daily schedule so I could play cards in the afternoon. It was not until about halfway through the voyage that I had the opportunity to have several meals with Dave and learn about his creativity and story that had led to a life where he could not only take his family on this trip but also financially support a nonprofit organization providing leadership and ethics training to youth across the country. I knew he was hugely invested in the organization's mission because his business card included its website and was a constant topic of our conversations. Toward the end of the voyage, he urged me to call on him if he could provide support in my professional life, especially knowing that I did not have a job to go back to in the United States.

I didn't think much of his offer but enjoyed the rest of the journey and developed a great relationship with the Bender family and the quirky card game that took the ship by storm. The day I returned to the States, I was on my friend's couch, my home as I began a job search, and randomly started looking for part-time positions on a nonprofit job site. One of the first postings I saw was for a data entry clerk for CHARACTER COUNTS!, which sounded familiar, but I couldn't figure out why. So I applied for the position, knowing that I was overqualified but also that the job fit my need for a part-time position while I also conducted a national job search. As I read more about the organization, I realized soon I had seen this organization's name on Dave's business card. Once I realized this connection, I sent him an e-mail to say hello and ask if he knew about this position and any contacts I could connect with or if he could put in a good word, which he gladly agreed to do. Dave replied with contact information, and I sent a personal e-mail to Justin, mentioning Dave and my interest in this position. Within a day, I got a call back from Justin to set up an interview and inquire further. I talked about my travels and what I had learned from Dave and why this position would be a great fit for the organization and me. Before I knew it, I had a part-time job working within an educational nonprofit, exploring a very different culture, developing a new network, and learning humility while being the best data entry specialist there is!

Concurrently, I was invited to an on-campus interview for the directorship of the UCLA LGBT Campus Resource Center, and in one of my conversations with Justin, I soon learned that he was a gay alumnus yet had not used the LGBT Center at all during his time on campus. Listening to his experience made me even more interested in this position so I could make a difference for future students like him. In our conversation, I also remembered that a year earlier I had met Peter, my ex-boyfriend's uncle who was gay, Asian, and a UCLA alumnus who had worked at UCLA for many years. Though my ex-partner and I were not in touch, I had become friends with his uncle and partner through social networking sites, and I took the risk of sending a message and asking him to share some of his experiences on LGBT climate and history on campus. I asked him to help identify key stakeholders and issues to consider in assessing a professional "fit," which gave me deeper insight into the campus politics and constituents and helped me develop ideas to navigate this system.

This conversation also reminded me that I had served on an executive board with someone who had actually worked in the center a few years earlier. We even roomed together at a conference, so I reached out to Emily, and she quickly responded with some critical information and freely shared her experience on campus. I also reached out to a mentor, whom I had met during a national conference, and asked to have coffee so she could give me advice on this interview. As I talked with her about my upcoming interview, she got excited and offered to connect me to a former student who was currently a staff member at UCLA so I could get a campus-based perspective on LGBT issues. This staff member offered to talk on the phone and was honest about campus culture, lingo, and approaches to student development, which greatly aided my process of developing a vision for how my experiences and skills could enhance the LGBT Center and identify areas of career growth.

By the end of the week, I felt quite confident I had done sufficient research and networking to feel comfortable going into my on-campus interviews. Once I was offered the position, I made sure to follow up with all these people to thank them for taking time to share their stories and vision with me.

A year later, I found myself at a Semester at Sea reunion for our voyage, playing cards with the Benders, talking about my new job and all the exciting aspects of the work. Though these people entered my life from various spaces, they were all critical in their own way to my career search and success in finding a perfect career fit. Networking and connecting is really just a fancy way of talking about relationships. When I meet people, I make sure we can find something in common, ask for a business card, and write something we spoke about on the card. If I am still thinking about a conversation a few weeks later, I send an e-mail to that person just to say hello and reconnect with that conversation. I also make sure I continue to stay connected via social media. This is not rocket science but about being present and aware and making genuine connections to foster relationships and unexpected opportunities.

Networking is about being at the right place at the right time, and if we are present, every moment can become that moment. I didn't develop any of these relationships for the sake of their network, but that was the by-product that helped me get to my current position. Go ahead, give it a try!

Chapter Summary

Bobby, Lindsey, Sara, Claudia, and Raja provide great examples of how you can utilize relationship building and political savvy in your overall career strategy. They also demonstrate that relationships sometimes cross the professional and personal divide, which illustrates how relationships of all types are valuable and you may establish professional connections in places or through channels that you never considered at first. This chapter gives you some ideas about how you can begin to cultivate relationships and navigate politics. The most important point is that relationships matter, and you must discover how you can build, maintain, and sustain them.

8

SELF-REFLECTION

With contributions by Brandon Bowden, merz lim,
becky martinez, Mary C. Medina, and Tanya O. Williams

Know thyself.

—Socrates

If we are too busy, if we are carried away every day by our projects,
our uncertainty, our craving, how can we have the time to stop
and look deeply into the situation—our own situation?

—Thich Nhat Hanh

Do You!

Similar to networking and connecting, the process of self-reflection is a very personal one. Each of us reflects in our own way. I tend to use multiple reflection approaches. First and foremost, expression and contemplation through writing—in a journal or a blog—have always been a go-to for me since I was a child. Getting the thoughts and feelings out of my head and onto a page (literal or figurative) is helpful for me. What is even more valuable about the process of writing for me is that it creates a log of my growth and development. It is always quite insightful to go back and reread my self-reflective writing days, or especially years, later. For example, I tend to examine the handwritten journals from my teen years when I visit my parents' house. It allows me to see myself through a different lens and to chart both how far I have come and which patterns of behavior or thought I am still sorting out. Furthermore, I enjoy how both big and small parts of my life are recorded and bring jolts of memories back to me that normally lie dormant in my mind. I am finding similar worth in my new approach of blogging. I can, with a few keystrokes and from any computer in the world, pull up a venue that provides me with not only an outlet for my thoughts but also a tool for context. Can you tell I enjoy and support this method of self-reflection?

Critically thinking about my past, my present, and my future is another tactic I employ, often while driving (not the safest idea, though), during plane flights, or throughout a run or time at the gym. Spending time in a serene location helps me. I define *serene* as beach or mountain locations—places that remind me of the vastness of the world and that I am a small part of a much larger whole. Listening to music helps me reflect too. There is just something about finding a song with lyrics that articulate my feelings that allows me to ponder life. Sharing with others and talking about things aloud rounds out my top approaches to reflection. When I have to explain things to others, it makes me think through a different lens and, ideally, see things from a new perspective. It also does not hurt to get a little feedback from my circle of friends and colleagues. But, those are things that work for me. You need to do you. So, if you do not already know, you will need to figure out which self-reflection practices work best for you.

Know Your Style

As mentioned, there are a multitude of methods that encourage self-reflection. The key is realizing which ones work for you. Learning your reflection style may take time and may involve a process of trial and error, especially if self-reflection is new to you. Try keeping a journal or personal blog (password protect that thing!). Take a walk in an area that provides you with a little peace; it could be around a lake, by an ocean, through the woods, or in your own neighborhood. Have a purposeful conversation with a colleague, partner, or friend. Divulge what is on your mind, and ask the other person to just listen and save the advice for another time. Turn on some tunes that speak to your soul. Spend some time in a rocking chair. Watch a movie or TV show in which you see some of your own life. Take a behavioral assessment (Myers-Briggs, StrengthsFinder, DiSC, etc.). Read a book that makes you question your beliefs or worldview. Turn off your mobile devices. Paint, draw, or create something. See what works. And, for whatever does not, at least you know that it does not work, and sometimes knowing what does not work is just as valuable as knowing what does.

Level of comfort. Every person has a different level of comfort when it comes to self-reflection. It is similar to a bell curve with the folks who really like it on one end, the folks who really do not on the other, and everyone else falling somewhere in the middle.

This kind of contemplation can make people uneasy because it can reveal some things they do not necessarily want to recognize. It can lead to people having to acknowledge both their strengths and accolades and their shortcomings and pitfalls. Reflection also has the ability to reveal patterns—patterns of thought, behavior, action, and reaction. And patterns are not always pretty. However, the more reflection you do, the more comfortable you will become with reflection and the learning that comes with it.

Context. When and how reflection occurs is significant. If self-reflection can be practiced in a proactive way, it is most advantageous. Proactive self-reflection allows for forward thinking and goal setting. You can use this to think about who you want to be as a person and professional, what you want to do, and how you plan to get there. For example, you would never have picked up this book (willingly or not) unless you had given some thought to a career in higher education or student affairs.

The catch is that imagining how something will go can lead to disappointment when things do not unfold as they did in your mind. For example, if you reflect on an upcoming conversation you are going to have with a colleague about a program that needs more planning and organization, you tend to imagine yourself saying this and your colleague saying that and the resolution being such and such. Then you have the dialogue. You say this, but your colleague does not say the "that" that you expected. This can lead to frustration and disappointment, shock, or disbelief. You may begin to think the reflection was not useful. That is false. The reflection of what you preferred to happen and what you think needed to happen is useful. Thinking you can forecast exactly how things will play out is not. Self-reflection is a tool to help you sift through your own emotions, thoughts, and behavior to determine what you want. It is not, however, a means of predicting the future.

It is also important to recognize that you will not often have the luxury to stop in the middle of something, like a critical conversation with a supervisor, and say, "Wait a second, I need to reflect on this and get back to you." Now, sometimes you do, and that is very helpful. But, many times, reflection is a reactive approach—looking back on the past and trying to make meaning of things. Self-reflection is a critical aspect of meaning-making and provides you with opportunities to make sense of and find solace in life's happenings.

Practice Makes Productive

As with many things in life, the more you practice self-reflection, the more comfort you will have with it, the more value you will get out of it, and the more productive of a process it will be for you.

I choose to say "practice makes productive" because the traditional "practice makes perfect" does not philosophically jive with me. In fact, the whole concept of perfection is not something I believe in anymore, which has been a major shift for me over the years. I used to strive for perfection and found myself always coming up a bit short. It was maddening. Then one day I heard a boss of mine describe the difference between excellence and perfection. He explained, "There is a difference between excellence and perfection. When you are working with people, there will never be perfection, because people aren't perfect. So strive for excellence." His words hit me to the core. All those years I had been striving for perfection when, in fact, it was unattainable. So why put myself through that? Why strive for something I could never achieve, when, instead, I could still make every effort to do a phenomenal job at something, allow room for things to go awry, move to Plan B, and still feel that I did excellent work? It makes more sense to me, now, to strive for excellence and to know that, inevitably, something is not going to go as planned. I can, therefore, cancel out the realization of perfection and have the flexibility and adaptability to keep going and maintain excellence.

The same is true for the practice of self-reflection. Perfection is not the aim. Rather, it is excellence and productivity. The more types of self-reflection you try, the closer you are to recognizing which methods work for you. The more times you contemplate, the easier it will be to ponder the next time. The more you hold yourself accountable to the practice of self-reflection, the more productive you will be at it and the more value it will bring to your career and your life.

Personal Stories

Self-reflection is a process and a practice distinct to the individual. What works for me may not work for you and vice versa. However, it can be helpful to hear how others practice self-reflection so you can gather ideas to try out in your own life. The following are the stories of five individuals—Brandon, merz, becky, Mary, and Tanya—who engage in the field of higher education. They share how they practice self-reflection in their careers and personal lives. Listen to their stories to find how they incorporate self-reflection tactics to make themselves better professionals and better people, and open your mind to their suggestions of how you can practice self-reflection.

Brandon's Story

What is self-reflection? According to *Merriam-Webster's* dictionary, *self-reflection* is the act of looking within oneself and examining one's own mental and emotional state and mental processes. Self-reflection is a common activity within my day-to-day routine as a student affairs administrator, whether it is in my role as an administrator in the student union, as an adjunct faculty member in the College of Education, or as a formal hearing officer for

Student Rights and Responsibilities. I use self-reflection as a strategy in my career to grow as an individual and also to ensure that I am being the best employee, supervisor, advisor, instructor, hearing officer, and mentor I can be.

I have three primary techniques that I use to be self-reflective. The first technique is the use of a personal journal. Although I do not write in my journal on a daily basis, I do write in it on at least a weekly basis and more in some weeks than in others, depending on the events of the week. The journal entries generally focus on an issue at work, a decision that I am struggling with, a proud moment with a student or staff member, or sometimes simply a mood that I am in. The thing I like most about my journal is that I can truly say anything without the fear or concern that I may get some adverse reaction or response. I can also bounce ideas around that don't quite make sense at the time, yet I don't have to explain myself any further to make it understandable to the outside world.

The second technique that I use is a series of formal and informal meetings with friends, students, colleagues, and mentors. It is not uncommon for me to grab colleagues after a meeting to ask them how they thought the meeting went, whether they thought I got my point across, or if I should have possibly approached something in a different way. I frequently ask for feedback on presentations I give, and when I am teaching, I have 5-minute debriefings after class with my teaching assistant to gauge how he thought class went, what he liked and didn't like, and if we need to do something differently. In my teaching, I also utilize with my students a technique called "Stop, Start, Continue" that I learned from a mentor. This is an opportunity for my students to give me feedback on what they want me to stop, start, or continue as it pertains to my teaching style or what we focus on for topics in class. I also use this technique from time to time in my journal as way to check in on myself.

The third technique that I use is a very simple one. On my way home from work each day, I purposefully avoid turning music on or making use of "hands-free" calling. This quiet time in the car for my 20-minute commute allows me some quality time to reflect on my day. During this time, I go through a series of questions in my head:

- How was my day?
- Knowing what I know now, what, if anything, would I do differently next time?
- What can I learn from this experience?
- What does this situation remind me of?

These questions help me to think a little deeper about what is going on around me, the impact I have on others, and the impact others have on me.

I utilize these techniques because I think that they are very important to career strategizing in the sense that it provides an opportunity to constantly gauge how I can do better and also how I can be better. I am a true believer that being aware of oneself is a critical step toward self-improvement. Self-reflection can be difficult for some people because it often forces the examination of the negative aspects of ourselves. Although it may be human nature to want to avoid seeing ourselves in a negative manner, only through the identification of our shortcomings are we able to move past them and progress toward our goals.

Self-reflection is also important to career strategizing because it can help you to determine where you are in life, where you want to be in terms of a career, and what the best path will be to get there. Without this self-reflection, you live reactively to the environment around you and not proactively from within for the best desired outcome. When you fail to self-reflect, it can cause you to be unsure of why you are doing what you do. For most of us in student affairs, self-reflection is essential in reminding us why we are in the field. It is usually because we had an experience, a mentor, or an advisor that made such a positive impact on us that we want to have the same positive impact on others. So in the end, self-reflection helps me to keep my focus on the end goal, which is to become a senior student affairs administrator.

Self-reflection is not natural for everyone and can be more work for some than others. I personally have always found it rather easy, simply because one of my personality traits is to be analytical. I like to know the meaning behind things and why things are the way they are, including myself. For those who don't find it as easy, I generally recommend starting out informally with a little reflection with friends and family as you eat a meal or on your drive to class or work. For those who feel that there simply is no time in the day to reflect, I suggest reflecting during otherwise mundane daily activities or just prior to going to sleep.

Reflecting is about thinking a little deeper and asking those questions that help the brain think. I have found that asking myself questions, such as what worked, what didn't work, and how can I be better, can serve as catalysts to help start my time of reflection. Although there are numerous other examples of self-reflection, these are a few that work for me and can, hopefully, help get you started.

merz's Story

I describe the process of my self-reflection as a pictorial image akin to a cartoon movie strip. This process could be from simple to complex thoughts or vice versa. Growing up I was in a single, narrow mind-set. Thoughts came and went; I did not make any conscious effort in analyzing what these musings meant. Those thoughts, however, never left and were merely compartmentalized in some area in my mind.

Through my college and graduate school years, I learned what self-reflection meant and what its significant meaning was in my day-to-day interactions. At the beginning stages, my process of self-reflection emerged through the exploration of my cultural identity and what being Asian and Filipino meant and what perceptions I portrayed to my friends and to the community.

Reflecting now, I see my cultural background played a large role in my process of self-reflection in that it limited my ability to ponder, or at least question, things that may appear unusual. I identify as a 1.5-generation (refers to people who immigrate to a new country before or during their early teens) Filipino immigrant to this country. As a child, I was expected to serve my parents and engage in good conduct where I was not to bring shame or any sort of attention to my family's name. I was taught to be loyal to my parents and elders, blindly obeying their authority and the conditions imposed in the family of a patriarchal system. I was taught that family and kinship is the foundation of any Filipino family—the individual belongs to the collective. As an obedient son, I followed expectations that were explicit.

The disagreement between my family and my own perceptions began when I sought membership in different school organizations and surrounded myself with other campus leaders whose ideas were not the "norm" of Filipino culture. I was blessed with mentors and student advisors who understood my young mind and saw the potential in me. Not only did these mentors push me to think outside the box, but they were also very cognizant of my cultural background and the unsaid expectations that were placed on me. Through their able hands and continued support, I created an environment where I allowed myself to openly express my thoughts and feelings without hesitation. From these relationships I was able to extend my connections and networks, even pursuing new avenues of self-reflection such as drawing or painting the emotions that were currently running through me to make meaning from them. I knew then that I too wanted to give back a supportive environment for any student. Thus, a pursuit of a student affairs degree was apparent in my future.

As I moved into furthering my education, I discovered the value of incorporating self-reflection and career aspirations into student affairs. Thus a research topic for graduate school was at hand. I knew grad school would be about two years, so I figured I might as well take the plunge of experiencing something different and far removed from the Texan life.

Prior to delving into college searches and personal statements, I knew that this chapter in my life had an expiration date of two years, so I chose to take this opportunity and explore another part of the country—toward independency and self-growth. I knew I was always welcomed at home if I decided to change my mind and come back. This time, moments of self-reflection were constant and at a peak. I was able to create three criteria that allowed me to decide on what programs I should be applying for: a non-GRE program, a mix of faculty and practitioners, and a guaranteed assistantship position. Historically, I did poorly on standardized testing, and I felt completing the GRE would not justify my ability to succeed in graduate school. Because both my parents have terminal degrees, searching for a school without a GRE requirement was again challenging the grain of their beliefs.

The makeup of faculty was another aspect that was important to me. Courses of study that revolved around theory, concepts, statistics, and research were not my idea of learning, and I knew I would face many struggles along the way. Because I am more of an experiential learner, receiving on-the-job training, utilizing internship programs, and shadowing practitioners who have taught the classes were more appealing to my palate. I felt the applied learning experiences would allow me to better understand the materials by experiencing it firsthand.

Being financially stable was another aspect I had to keep in mind, as I went through undergrad having to pay for my own studies through loans and scholarships. This meant a guaranteed graduate assistantship would need to be included in the package of whatever program I was accepted to.

These pieces became the deciding factors in my quest for graduate school. Deep in my heart I wanted to show my parents, especially my mom, that I would be able to succeed.

In the end, the University of Connecticut (UConn) came out on top. UConn's program encompassed all the requirements I put forth to meet. The program viewed the applicant as a whole, maintained a collaborative department with student affairs professionals and professors, and offered the opportunity to further explore my cultural identity working as a graduate assistant at the Asian American Cultural Center.

By mapping out and identifying specific requirements, I was able to visually see the experiences and skills I was trying to attain in my studies.

It was my own ethnic identity and assistantship that validated the functional area that I wanted to pursue in my career as a student affairs professional. In serving the Asian American Cultural Center, I am able not only to mentor students but also to challenge them to think critically. I am able to share similar experiences of coming to terms with my own identity as Asian and American. My experiences through my own reflections were fundamental to my becoming able to push my students to a level of inquiry about their own identity, for most an uncharted place. I cannot express the amount of gratitude that I attain from being able to help provide support to these students and delve into topics that revolve around "what it is like to be Asian American." It is a powerful experience seeing similar transformations occur in students. A reflex response I have for students would be, "I went through a familiar experience as an undergraduate student." This is an impetus to continue to be challenged as I see and discover other Asian American students undergo the same struggles.

As I continue to learn and grow within this field, my process of reflection runs through a gamut of things: events, places, and people, usually sparked by a series of questions—questions that revolve around social injustice and inequality. At times these questions unearthed a deeper unresolved inner conflict that has had a continuing influence on me. Usually the first couple of questions that I ask myself are, "What led me to feel this way?" and "How can I move to a better place?" These questions alone have been useful to allow me to deconstruct and funnel my thoughts into a more refined process of self-reflection. I will state that, at times, posing these questions has left me paralyzed and quiet because of pain and insecurities. However, in my current stage in life, I can muster the courage and accept these difficult questions for what they are right now without feeling stunned.

As I presented these questions to myself, I started to write these thoughts down into a personal blog (whether it was done in English or my native dialect). I recorded my thoughts through my cell phone and replayed it over and over. Yes, at first I felt awkward professing some of my innermost thoughts; at times, it led me to dark places and left me with an unsettling feeling. Nonetheless, the process of self-reflection is cathartic, as if something had been lifted from my shoulders—the burden of unwanted stress, that "aha moment." That profound (well, this is subjective) insight toward myself, a realization of an abstract idea that has now been conceptualized into something concrete, a means to an end. One of the smart things I did was to seek out trusted colleagues I am able to use as a sounding board for triggering events. They, in turn, were not afraid to ask difficult questions to help me understand the root cause of my feelings. This process allowed me to remain true to myself rather than hide behind other people's "truths" or "beliefs."

Engaging in these activities took time, and it was a very slow process—a continuous battle between me and the second me. In this process, however, I learned how I really was, learning who I really am—addressing my weaknesses and learning how to address them, my gifts and how to use them. The greatest thing I learned was "to be true to me." Finding and accepting the truth about myself is liberating. Accepting that it was okay to be emotional and be more trusting in the process than the outcome. I truly believe there is no right or wrong way of portraying yourself. It is more important to be willing to open yourself up and explore the creative landscape of your mind. This is the process of self-reflection. Now, I welcome triggers. I welcome nice thoughts and even the not so nice ones. I can face them; they are mere thoughts and I should say, "Maybe they are just like the cartoon characters in my mind."

becky's Story

This morning I went for a run, and throughout most of it I was filled with curiosity and gratitude. Somewhere around mile two I came across three women younger than I am, with one seeming to stare as I ran by. I instantly thought to myself, "How did I get to this place in life compared to these women who will probably be trapped in this life circumstance?" I was over-taken with a slew of wonderings and questions.

What I failed to mention is that I was running in a low-income mobile home community with clear visible poverty, and I understood this life cir-cumstance, as it was once mine. Well, maybe not the clear visible poverty; however, the more I understand social justice and am in self-reflection about my childhood, the more I learn about my working-class poor background.

Although I do not know their personal stories, I am keen enough to understand their surroundings and the data that speak to their life trajectory. I hope they too will find a way to disrupt the dominant narrative of their surroundings, and yet I sadly know that is a rare occurrence. I also think about Paulo Freire's work in that they may not know any different type of life, which usually results in continuing the cycle of oppression and all that accompanies it.

I name gratitude because I am able to run at 7:30 a.m. when most people are heading to work. In fact, by this time all of my adult family has been at work for an hour if not a few. Although I indeed work, when I am not on the road I have opportunities afforded to very few people. In addition, I am able to physically run without needing to think about it beyond the weather dic-tating what I will wear, and because I live in Southern California, that usually means choosing between a short-sleeve shirt and a long-sleeve shirt. Last, I am in deep gratitude for the time and space during a run to clear my mind and focus on whatever enters my space. The time is filled with self-reflection of my immediate life issues, or of the many bold possibilities to transform the world, or simply about how to mentally make it through the last mile.

Self-reflection comes in various forms from those scheduled and routine (e.g., journaling at a specific time of the day) to spontaneous happenstance (e.g., coming across strangers on a morning run). It may be part of the yearly professional performance review, a necessary component for deciding where to live, or pondering one of my favorite questions: Today, am I being the person I strive to be? Regardless of the modality of self-reflection, I have found it necessary for my authentic growth and development.

The practice and skill of self-reflection bring clarity and a sense of calm to our, many times, chaotic and busy lives. It can be said that taking time for self-reflection is similar to creating a habit of exercising for a healthy life. The more it becomes a part of our daily routine, the more powerfully it will impact our lives and has the propensity to transform us. I intentionally spend at least 15 minutes a day in some form of self-reflection. It is what I often refer to as "becky time," and it took me years to realize its importance in my life.

Over time I discovered daily journaling does not work for me even though I enjoy and appreciate a beautiful journal. I occasionally use one for documentation of life events, which usually leads to some self-reflection. Instead of journaling, I spend a great deal of time in deep thought and emotion about my critical, and sometimes not so critical, life context and content. This includes my relationship with self, family, and friends to my life's work with social justice to how I spend my time. As silly as it seems, I spend time thinking of ways I would spend a lottery winning. This helps me gain clarity of my priorities, leading me to focus my time and energy on those aspects of life. It also pushes me out of my task-driven routine and enables me to dream big.

The other form of self-reflection that meets my needs is connection with a handful of friends who are my go-to people. I am able to process with them, which includes honest feedback and leads to challenging, soul-provoking questions. For the record, moments in these conversations are rough and uncomfortable, and it is at this juncture I have developed the most. During a difficult time in my last administrative position, a friend asked me, "What would your life look like if you weren't afraid?" This was the impetus for some very real, crucial conversations with my go-to people regarding my career. As a result, I found the courage to change my path to doing what is congruent to my values, fills my soul, and utilizes my skills and talents. These sacred relationships took years to form and nurture and are filled with trust, vulnerability, and care. I am infinitely grateful for this cadre, as they are my self-reflection coaches who guide me to better understand myself.

Through self-reflection, I am more grounded in my values and on the continuous road of self-discovery and transformation. I think this perspective is on the pendulum of either ancient philosophy or new age thinking. Whatever the frame, I am a better consultant, auntie, friend, practitioner, educator, and overall person as a result of self-reflection. This practice allows me to continue reinventing myself to be more powerful and humble in living my daily question: Today, am I being the person I strive to be?

Mary's Story

Who am I? MBTI identifies me as an ISFJ: Introversion, Sensing, Feeling, and Judging. StrengthsFinder reveals my top five strengths as Discipline, Empathy, Futuristic, Harmony, and Relator. My DISC Classic behavioral pattern is Perfectionist, with Conscientiousness being my highest dimension of behavior. All of these self-assessment tools reveal characteristics and personality traits about myself and serve as a part of my self-reflection process. These assessments help me understand the characteristics that I embody that blend into my professional working style and how I interact with those around me. In reviewing the descriptions of these self-assessment tools, I find myself agreeing with the results. Yes, I am an introverted personality, and I have a keen desire for details. I also get a better understanding of the strengths and challenges related to these characteristics, as well as many others. It's important for me to trust in my strengths and apply them to my benefit and also to manage my challenges. This is facilitated through a process of self-reflection.

I frequently sit down and think about where I've been and where I want to go. My identities as a Latina female and first-generation college student have played a significant role in my determination to succeed. Although I began my college journey with no aspirations beyond a baccalaureate degree, I have now transitioned into someone pursuing a doctoral degree. I have several goals for the future and am making steady progress toward achieving them. Rarely does anything ever just happen overnight. Therefore, I like to frequently take time to reflect on the past, present, and future.

There are three primary ways I like to use to reflect. As I am an introverted person, the first way usually happens solitarily. While I'm at home on a quiet afternoon, I'll find myself getting lost in my thoughts. I think about my educational and professional experiences. This type of self-reflection tends to happen instinctively for me. I continue to celebrate the various things I have achieved and make plans for the future. I often find myself jotting down ideas and my vision for the future on a random piece of paper or in a journal. My exploration tends to work the best and the most naturally when I simply put pen to paper and see what comes out. I don't necessarily create a step-by-step plan of how to get there, but I list items to accomplish along the way. I then put the piece of paper or journal somewhere for safekeeping so I can revisit it at a later date to check my progress.

A second way I like to reflect is by talking with my friends, colleagues, and mentors in higher education. From new professionals to senior-level administrators, individuals within higher education have had very differing paths to get where they are now. Often, the hardest thing for me to remember is that there is no one correct way to get to where you want to go.

As an individual who studied mathematical sciences in college, I find this is often the most challenging concept for me. At times I am still accustomed to formulaic ways of thinking about things. If I ultimately want to become a senior-level administrator, what must I do to get there? For the most part, the answer is I can get there any way I want. Although not necessarily formulaic, this has become an exciting part of my career, as I get to determine what experiences I want to gain. I often reflect on professional competencies in the field to help guide my path, which has inspired me to get practical experience and exposure to multiple functional areas within student affairs. The professional competencies are those informally learned from colleagues and those formally developed such as the *Professional Competency Areas for Student Affairs Practitioners* jointly created by ACPA and NASPA Joint Task Force on Professional Competencies (2010).

The third way I choose to reflect is by attending conferences. I strongly believe that involvement in professional associations and attendance at professional conferences provides a great opportunity for professional development. It never fails that while I'm attending a conference I feel an overwhelming desire to reflect on my career ambitions. I'm able to interact with student affairs administrators at all different levels in the field. I also have an opportunity to reconnect with colleagues, classmates, and friends who are working in different functional areas at varying levels at institutions across the nation. Being in such an environment provides me with encouragement and motivation to strive for my ultimate career goals. This is when I usually create a list of goals for the upcoming year. These range from experiences I want to obtain at work to educational pursuits.

There are also times in which my self-reflection becomes a blend of all of the aforementioned strategies. An example of when I used self-reflection to guide my career is when I explored the idea of presenting at a national conference. It was 2010, and I had recently attended the NASPA annual conference. The programs I attended and conversations I had with my colleagues again put me in a mode of reflecting on my career ambitions. I had several experiences presenting but not on a national level. I felt like this would be something to strengthen my professional skills and help me with my career ambitions. So I began writing down ideas of topics to discuss and potential copresenters. I made it a goal to submit at least three programs for a national conference that next year. Ultimately, I achieved my goal and had two programs accepted at the 2011 NASPA annual conference. I was able to return to my notes and mark off my achievement.

Overall, my self-reflection strategy takes on multiple forms throughout the year. It helps me make a draft plan of where I want to go in my career. I've learned that throughout self-reflection, it is important to allow for flexibility.

Everything doesn't always happen the way you plan, and this can serve as either a disappointment or a pleasant surprise. However, every experience is full of learning opportunities. There are opportunities to see the positives and negatives of each situation. It is important to learn from the experiences and to use them to make a beneficial change for the future. It is important to set short-term and long-term goals. But it is also important to not let these goals keep you from unanticipated opportunities that come your way. As long as you have a determined spirit, you can create action and succeed.

Tanya's Story

I, like many other student affairs folks, was "overinvolved" during my undergraduate years. As an African American woman at a large, predominantly White, public, southern institution, I believe it was my way of not dealing with the racism and sexism that came at me daily, while also not having to deal with my own internalized oppression. While at the same time avoiding all of those harmful outgrowths of a nation that even then failed to talk openly about social identity, I found myself involved with organizations that wanted to educate others about diversity and build bridges between our different identities. Though I was involved in the school's newspaper, its public television station (both of which because I was a journalism major), orientation, programming board, and many other activities, my work with diversity education fueled me in different ways. Though I was not as aware of the reason at the time, the diversity education work allowed for my often-overlooked racial and socioeconomic identity to be seen and talked about at a predominantly White institution. It gave me an opportunity to talk about the differences that I noticed, to help build bridges across those differences, and to find a place where I could be all of myself. It was a fateful day when I found myself in my diversity education organization advisor's office and she revealed that I could get paid to do what she did and, more so, there was a graduate degree that I could obtain that would allow me to work with students for the rest of my life.

Fast-forward almost 20 years; my self-reflection about being fed by work in diversity education—now called social justice education—has led to a nontraditional student affairs career and currently a role as a deputy vice president of institutional diversity and community engagement at a seminary in New York City. My heart will always be centered on student engagement and working with students (both undergraduate and, now, graduate students), but I also have come to understand that when you are in the role of a student affairs social justice educator, the impact that you can have on changing campus culture is limited if your role is limited to providing programming for students, as students are on campus for only a limited amount of time. I have shifted my perspective to include social justice education and cultural competency for all constituencies on university and seminary campuses.

The beginning of my career in social justice student affairs work was not an easy one. During the mid-90s, the roles of diversity educator or multicultural director were not as plentiful as they are now. While my graduate school cohort members, who were venturing into residence life or student programming, had interview after interview scheduled during our job search semester, I applied to fewer jobs and was invited on fewer interviews. But I didn't give up hope. I knew that my want to do social justice work was an internal calling and not just a career or a job. The location (higher education) where I was able to do my social justice work was a great location, but I believe that I would be doing the work of educating about oppression, building communities, teaching communication skills, and working toward equity because it is a reflection of what moves me.

Because of that internal knowing, my path in higher education has looked a little different. After obtaining a master's of higher education administration and working in diversity education with undergraduate students for five years, I decided it was time to further my education and work toward a doctorate. Traditionally, many student affairs professionals get doctorates in higher education administration, leadership development, or organizational leadership. Again, because of my call to social justice change, I found the first social justice education program in the country and obtained my doctorate in that field. My commitment to service in higher education continued, but I wanted a sharper understanding of the issues that I wanted to see changed in the world. In that program, my ability to reflect and to understand myself and my impact on the world improved, and it not only made me a stronger social justice educator but also made me a stronger student affairs professional. I can recall during my second year in the social justice education program we actually had a class called "Self Awareness in Social Justice Education," which clarified for me that I would never be able to avoid self-reflection if I wanted to do effective work in this field. I had long been a "journaler," keeping a regular personal journal throughout college and continuing throughout my life, but this work was going to require me to continue to reflect about not only my feelings but also my identities, my impact on others, and their impact on me. Strengthening my skills of communication and understanding my social location in society as a result of my social identities, I can better connect with students, faculty, staff, and administration. In addition, it encouraged me to look at the organizational nature of higher education and determine the impact that I was able to have versus the impact I wanted to have. Throughout my master's work, I was determined to eventually reach the level of VP of student affairs because that was the role that I was "supposed" to want. Listening more closely to my own call and noticing the places where I got the most energy—and watching higher education transform as my years in the field inched forward—I let go of that "supposed to" and set my sights on a role where I would have the kind of impact that I wanted to have: chief diversity officer.

That's the role I find myself in today. And to say I "find myself in" is belittling the years of reflecting, listening, trusting, and risk taking that it took to get here. I think I have taken for granted the practice of self-reflection that I have developed, because it feels very second nature to me now. The moments that I sit quietly during my Sunday morning reflection and journal writing have become a ritual for me. Questions come to me as I ride the subway or as I sit in meetings, and I write them down and hold on to them mentally (sometimes for months) until a clearer answer surfaces internally. I also self-reflect as I have conversations with students and colleagues; the questions they ask or the questions I ask give as much information about me and my thinking as the response that I give. Silencing the noise of life around me encourages me to go inside and check out my internal voice to make sure my actions and values line up consistently. I can now tell very clearly when I am inconsistent or feeling "off" because of my practice and value of self-reflection and analysis. The self-reflection that I have engaged in throughout my life helps me to know that I am in the right field because I love my work—and still consider myself a student affairs professional. Ultimately, the work that I do in my role is still aimed at students having the best experience at the institution that they have chosen to attend. The only thing is now I don't work only with and for students anymore. I work with the whole institution, for the benefit of students, and, ultimately, for the people they will impact in the future.

Chapter Summary

Brandon, merz, becky, Mary, and Tanya provide great examples of how you can incorporate self-reflection into your overall career strategy. They also demonstrate that professional reflection and personal reflection are sometimes one and the same and that contemplation can occur at any time and in any place. This chapter gives you some ideas of how self-reflection can be performed, but the most important point is to know that reflection, regardless of the method used, is an individualized process that must be practiced—frequently and fervently.

APPENDIX A: INITIAL SELF-REFLECTION QUESTIONS

Take a few minutes to self-reflect on the following questions about your career.

What are my career goals for 1, 3, 5, 10 years from now? What is my ultimate career goal? (Or, to whose job on campus do I aspire, and why? How would I go about making myself qualified for that job?)

What kinds of educational credentials (formal and informal) do I have? Will my current education level get me to my career goal or ideal job?

What experiences and skill sets, both job related and volunteer, do I currently have on my résumé? Are there experiences and skills that I think I need in addition to those?

Do I have a professional development plan? Do I know how to create one?

Am I comfortable with networking or connecting? Why or why not? What strategies do I normally use in networking or connecting?

Do I frequently take time to reflect on my career? Do I assess where I am and where I would like to be and adjust my time and experiences to reflect my goals? What strategies can I use to reflect?

APPENDIX B: JOB INTERVIEW QUESTION EXAMPLES

Phone Interviews

- Why are you interested in this position and this institution, and how do they fit into your long-term goals?
- What experiences have you had that prepare you for this position?
- How do you establish trust and build relationships with students?
- What does a typical week look like for you in your current job? What do you enjoy, and what do you find challenging?
- Give us an example of a time that you were asked to manage multiple priorities within a position. What strategies did you use, and what was the outcome?
- Please describe your advising style.
- How would you approach a position such as this during your first month and 6 months?
- Do you have any additional questions for us?

On-Campus Interviews

Search Committee

- Why are you interested in this position and this university? How do they match your personal and career goals?
- Tell us about your experiences in student affairs.
- What do you hope to learn from this position?
- As an advisor or supervisor, describe to us how you would handle a crisis situation.
- How would you make the transition into an organization?
- How do you like to be supervised?
- Give an example of a time when you managed an event and needed to consider risk management.
- What is your philosophy on accountability? Please tell us about a time when you had to hold someone accountable.
- How do you manage your time, particularly when you have multiple priorities?

- How do you manage conflict between others and yourself? How do you mediate conflict among others?
- What questions do you have for us?

Students

- Please share with us what you currently know about this university and why you are interested in working with our department.
- What makes you a good candidate for this position?
- How do you handle stressful situations? Please share an example of a recent stressful situation you overcame.
- What is your approach to teamwork?
- Describe your ideal relationship with the students with whom you work.
- How do you motivate others?
- Give an example of a time in the past when you resolved a conflict.
- Please share an example of a time you had to think on your feet and react quickly.
- How will you build trust with students and colleagues?
- What questions do you have for us?

Colleagues

- Tell us why you are interested in this position.
- How do you build trust with students?
- What are you looking for in colleagues? Your supervisor? How would your current colleagues and supervisor describe you?
- With what type of team do you work best? Please share an example of a work team you have found success with in the past.
- How does this position fit within your career goals?
- What role do you usually assume in a team?
- What will be your greatest challenges in this position?
- Describe your ability to develop strong relationships, particularly with departmental colleagues.
- What questions do you have for us?

Director Staff

- What excites you about this position?
- Describe your leadership style.
- Describe a time when you had a difficult decision to make, and discuss how you made that decision.

- What does diversity or social justice mean to you? Please share some examples that demonstrate your commitment to diversity or social justice.
- Cite a situation where you were faced with a supervisory challenge, and describe how you met that challenge.
- How do you hold students accountable? Please share an example.
- What motivates you?
- In August, we will hit the ground running with a variety of programs and functions. What will you do to learn, integrate yourself into the organization, and begin implementing your role?
- How will you help facilitate learning opportunities for the students with whom you work?
- How do you define *conflict*? Give a recent example that demonstrates your style of conflict management.
- What questions do you have for us?

Reference Checks

- In what capacity have you known the applicant and for how long?
- How would you describe the applicant's work in terms of quality, style, and ethic?
- How would you describe the applicant's style of relating to others?
- How well does the applicant develop trust and rapport with students?
- What are the applicant's greatest strengths or job skills?
- What are the applicant's areas of development?
- Is there anything else you would like to tell me about the applicant's work performance or behavior?
- If you had the opportunity, would you hire or rehire the applicant?

APPENDIX C: PROFESSIONAL DEVELOPMENT PLAN

Using the five career strategy components, create a professional development plan for yourself in the next year. Include any dates, deadlines, and timelines that you believe would be applicable.

Skills I Want to Strengthen and Acquire

Lifelong Learning Options

Include topics and areas to explore through reading and research, course work, conferences, meetings, and so on.

Committee, Presentation, Teaching, Volunteer, or Job Experiences to Pursue

Networking or Connection Tactics to Try; People With Whom I Want to Network or Connect

Self-Reflection Ideas

REFERENCES

ACPA. (2007). *New professionals needs study*. Washington, DC: Author.

ACPA and NASPA Joint Task Force on Professional Competencies. (2010). *Professional competency areas for student affairs practitioners*. Washington, DC: Author.

American Council on Education. (2013). *Report finds demographics of college graduates do not reflect changes in overall student body*. Retrieved from http://www.acenet.edu/news-room/Pages/Demographics-of-College-Graduates.aspx

Cuyjet, M. J., Longwell-Grice, R., & Molina, E. (2009). Perceptions of new student affairs professionals and their supervisors regarding the application of competencies learned in preparation programs. *Journal of College Student Development, 50*(1), 104–119.

Fenske, R. H. (1989). Evolution of student services profession. In U. Delworth & G. Hanson (Eds.), *Student services: A handbook for the profession* (2nd ed., pp. 25–56). San Francisco, CA: Jossey-Bass.

Hirt, J. (2006). *Where you work matters*. Lanham, MD: United Press of America.

Hoover, E. (2013, June 18). Demographic change doesn't mean the sky's falling. *The Chronicle of Higher Education*. Retrieved from http://chronicle.com/blogs/headcount/demographic-change-doesnt-mean-the-skys-falling/35223

Lawlor Group. (2013). *Ten trends for 2013: How marketplace conditions will influence private higher education enrollment—and how colleges can respond*. Retrieved from http://www.thelawlorgroup.com/pov/more-intelligence/lawlor-trends-2013

Renn, K., & Hodges, J. (2007). The first year on the job: Experiences of new professionals in student affairs. *NASPA Journal, 44*(2), 367–391.

Strategy. (n.d.). In *Merriam-Webster's online dictionary*. Retrieved from http://www.merriam-webster.com/dictionary/strategy

Tull, A. (2006). Synergistic supervision, job satisfaction, and intention to turnover of new professionals in student affairs. *Journal of College Student Development, 47*(4), 465–480.

Tull, A., Hirt, J. B., & Saunders, S. A. (2009). *Becoming socialized in student affairs administration: A guide for new professionals and their supervisors*. Sterling, VA: Stylus.

Waple, J. N. (2006). An assessment of skills and competencies necessary for entry-level student affairs work. *NASPA Journal, 43*(1), 1–18.

READING SUGGESTIONS FOR NEW AND MID-LEVEL STUDENT AFFAIRS EDUCATORS FROM YOUR PEERS

Books

Amey, J., & Reesor, L. (2009). *Beginning your journey: A guide for new professionals in student affairs*. Washington, DC: National Association of Student Personnel Administrators.

> The transition from graduate school to a full-time position in student affairs can be filled with both opportunities and challenges. To be successful, new professionals must understand the organizational and political realities of working on college and university campuses. *Beginning Your Journey: A Guide for New Professionals in Student Affairs* addresses the most critical and current issues for those entering the field of higher education.

Arbinger Institute. (2006). *The anatomy of peace: Resolving the heart of conflict*. San Francisco, CA: Berrett-Koehler.

> What if conflicts at home, conflicts at work, and conflicts in the world stem from the same root cause? And what if individually and collectively we systematically misunderstand that cause and unwittingly perpetuate the very problems we think we are trying to solve? Through an intriguing story of parents struggling with their troubled children and with their own personal problems, *The Anatomy of Peace* shows how to get past the preconceived ideas and self-justifying reactions that keep us from seeing the world clearly and dealing with it effectively.

Arbinger Institute. (2010). *Leadership and self-deception: Getting out of the box*. San Francisco, CA: Berrett-Koehler.

> Through a story everyone can relate to about a man facing challenges on the job and in his family, the authors of *Leadership and Self-Deception* expose the fascinating ways that we can blind ourselves to our true motivations and unwittingly sabotage the effectiveness of our own efforts to achieve success and increase happiness.

Belsky, G. (2010). *Why smart people make big money mistakes and how to correct them: Lessons from the life-changing science of behavioral economics*. New York, NY: Simon & Schuster.

In this fascinating and practical manual, Gary Belsky and Thomas Gilovich look at the ways we spend, save, borrow, invest, and waste money and reveal the psychology underlying irrational financial behavior. Entertaining case studies illustrate common patterns of thinking and show readers how changing their habits can protect and grow their assets.

Belsky, S. (2010). *Making ideas happen: Overcoming the obstacles between vision and reality.* New York, NY: Portfolio.

According to productivity expert Scott Belsky, no one is born with the ability to drive creative projects to completion. Execution is a skill that must be developed by building your organizational habits and harnessing the support of your colleagues. Although many of us focus on generating and searching for great ideas, Belsky shows why it's better to develop the capacity to make ideas happen—a capacity that endures over time.

Brown, B. (2012). *Daring greatly: How the courage to be vulnerable transforms the way we live, love, parent, and lead.* New York, NY: Gotham Books.

In *Daring Greatly*, Dr. Brown challenges everything we think we know about vulnerability. On the basis of 12 years of research, she argues that vulnerability is not weakness but rather our clearest path to courage, engagement, and meaningful connection. *Daring Greatly* sparks a new spirit of truth—and trust—in our organizations, families, schools, and communities.

Cain, S. (2012). *Quiet: The power of introverts in a world that can't stop talking.* New York, NY: Crown.

In *Quiet*, Susan Cain argues that we dramatically undervalue introverts and shows how much we lose in doing so. She charts the rise of the Extrovert Ideal throughout the twentieth century and explores how deeply it has come to permeate our culture. She also introduces us to successful introverts, from a witty, high-octane public speaker who recharges in solitude after his talks to a record-breaking salesman who quietly taps into the power of questions. *Quiet* has the power to permanently change how we see introverts and, equally important, how they see themselves.

Cullen, M. (2008). *35 dumb things well-intended people say: Surprising things we say that widen the diversity gap.* Garden City, NY: Morgan James.

Have you ever heard yourself or someone else say, "Some of my best friends are [Black, White, Asian, etc.]"? "I don't think of you as [gay, disabled, Jewish, etc.]"? "I don't see color, I'm color-blind"? These statements and dozens like them can build a divide between the people with whom we interact and us. Though well intended, language choices often widen the diversity gap, sometimes causing irreparable harm personally and professionally. If you've ever wanted to be more effective in your communication with others or have been afraid of saying the wrong thing, then this concise guide is essential to becoming more inclusive and diversity smart.

Duhigg, C. (2012). *The power of habit: Why we do what we do in life and business.* New York, NY: Random House.

At its core, *The Power of Habit* contains an exhilarating argument: The key to exercising regularly, losing weight, raising exceptional children, becoming more productive, building revolutionary companies and social movements, and achieving success is understanding how habits work. Habits aren't destiny. As Charles Duhigg shows, by harnessing this new science, we can transform our businesses, our communities, and our lives.

Frankl, V. (1992). *Man's search for meaning: An introduction to logotherapy.* Cutchogue, NY: Buccaneer Books.

On the basis of his own experience and the experiences of others he treated later in his practice, Frankl argues that we cannot avoid suffering, but we can choose how to cope with it, find meaning in it, and move forward with renewed purpose. Frankl's theory—known as logotherapy, from the Greek word *logos* ("meaning")—holds that our primary drive in life is not pleasure, as Freud maintained, but the discovery and pursuit of what we personally find meaningful.

Friere, P. (2000). *Pedagogy of the oppressed.* New York, NY: Continuum.

This text argues that the ignorance and lethargy of the poor are the direct result of the whole economic, social, and political domination. The book suggests that in some countries the oppressors use the system to maintain a "culture of silence." By using the right kind of education, the book suggests, avoiding authoritarian teacher-pupil models, and using the actual experiences of students and the continual shared investigation, every human being, no matter how impoverished or illiterate, can develop a new awareness of self and the right to be heard.

Glei, J. (2013). *Manage your day-to-day: Build your routine, find your focus, and sharpen your creative mind.* Las Vegas, NV: Amazon Publishing.

Are you overextended, overdistracted, and overwhelmed? Do you work at a breakneck pace all day, only to find that you haven't accomplished the most important things on your agenda when you leave the office? The world has changed, and the way we work has to change, too. With wisdom from 20 leading creative minds, *Manage Your Day-to-Day* will give you a tool kit for tackling the new challenges of a 24/7, always-on workplace.

Hersh, R., Merrow, J., & Wolfe, T. (2005). *Declining by degrees: Higher education at risk.* New York, NY: Palgrave Macmillan.

In *Declining by Degrees*, leading authors and educators such as Tom Wolfe, Jim Fallows, and Jay Mathews provide us with a valuable understanding of the serious issues facing colleges today, such as budget cuts, grade inflation, questionable recruitment strategies, and a major focus on Big Time Sports. Tied to the PBS documentary of the same name, *Declining by Degrees* creates a national discussion about the future of higher education and what we can do about it.

hooks, b. (2000). *Where we stand: Class matters.* New York, NY: Routledge.

Drawing on both her roots in Kentucky and her adventures with Manhattan Coop boards, bell hooks's *Where We Stand* is a successful Black woman's reflection—personal, straightforward, and rigorously honest—on how our dilemmas of class and race are intertwined and how we can find ways to think beyond them.

Lencioni, P. (2002). *The five dysfunctions of a team: A leadership fable.* San Francisco, CA: Jossey-Bass.

Throughout the story, Lencioni reveals the five dysfunctions that go to the very heart of why teams, even the best ones, often struggle. He outlines a powerful model and actionable steps that can be used to overcome these common hurdles and build a cohesive, effective team. Just as with his other books, Lencioni has written a compelling fable with a powerful yet deceptively simple message for all those who strive to be exceptional team leaders.

Lencioni, P. (2004). *Death by meeting: A leadership fable—about solving the most painful problem in business.* San Francisco, CA: Jossey-Bass.

Best-selling author Patrick Lencioni provides readers with another powerful and thought-provoking book, this one centered on a cure for the most painful yet underestimated problem of modern business: bad meetings. And what he suggests is both simple and revolutionary. *Death by Meeting* is nothing short of a blueprint for leaders who want to eliminate waste and frustration among their teams and create environments of engagement and passion.

Lencioni, P. (2007). *The three signs of a miserable job: A fable for managers (and their employees).* San Francisco, CA: Jossey-Bass.

Patrick Lencioni takes on a topic that almost everyone can relate to: the causes of a miserable job. Millions of workers, even those who have carefully chosen careers based on true passions and interests, dread going to work, suffering each day as they trudge to jobs that make them cynical, weary, and frustrated. It is a simple fact of business life that any person in any job, from investment banker to dishwasher, can become miserable. Through the story of a CEO turned pizzeria manager, Lencioni reveals the three elements that make work miserable—irrelevance, immeasurability, and anonymity—and gives managers and their employees the keys to make any job more fulfilling.

MacKenzie, G. (1998). *Orbiting the giant hairball: A corporate fool's guide to surviving with grace*. New York, NY: Penguin Group.

Creativity is crucial to business success. But too often, even the most innovative organization quickly becomes a "giant hairball"—a tangled, impenetrable mass of rules, traditions, and systems, all based on what worked in the past—that exercises an inexorable pull into mediocrity. This is a must-read for any manager looking for new ways to invigorate employees and for any professional who wants to achieve his or her best, most self-expressive, most creative, and fulfilling work.

Magolda, P., & Carnaghi, J. (2004). *Job one: Experiences of new professionals in student affairs*. Dallas, TX: American College Personnel Association.

In *Job One*, editors Peter Magolda and Jill Carnaghi place new professionals' stories center stage. The book focuses on nine narratives written by new professionals about their introduction and transitions into student affairs work. These stories document the joys and angst felt as new professionals prepare to transition from graduate school to work, search for their first student affairs position, assimilate campus norms, formulate a professional identity, satisfy supervisors' expectations, mediate cultural conflicts, and remain true to their personal and professional values. This book is a useful resource inviting new professionals, supervisors, and faculty to think differently about the ongoing education and needs of new professionals and offers a new perspective for optimizing new professionals' experiences.

McClellan, G., Stringer, J., & associates. (2009). *The handbook of student affairs administration*. San Francisco, CA: Jossey-Bass.

What issues and trends affect higher education and student affairs today? In this fully updated handbook, leading experts discuss the answer to this and other essential questions. They provide a definitive reference for student affairs professionals at all levels of administration and management.

The handbook offers specific, practical advice and broad approaches to planning and problem solving. It contains modernized discussions on such critical topics as institutional mission, institutional governance, understanding campus environments, finance and budgeting, assessment, program planning, staff selection, training and evaluation, and much more.

Pink, D. (2009). *Drive: The surprising truth about what motivates us.* New York, NY: Riverhead Books.
Most people believe that the best way to motivate is with rewards like money—the carrot-and-stick approach. That's a mistake, says Daniel H. Pink. In this provocative and persuasive book, he asserts that the secret to high performance and satisfaction—at work, at school, and at home—is the deep human need to direct our own lives, to learn and create new things, and to do better by ourselves and our world.

Ratey, J. (2013). *Spark: The revolutionary new science of exercise and the brain.* New York, NY: Little, Brown.
In *Spark*, John Ratey, MD, embarks upon a fascinating journey through the mind-body connection, illustrating that exercise is truly our best defense against everything from depression to ADD to addiction to menopause to Alzheimer's. Filled with amazing case studies (such as the revolutionary fitness program in Naperville, Illinois, that has put the local school district of 19,000 kids first in the world of science test scores), *Spark* is the first book to explore comprehensively the connection between exercise and the brain. It will change forever the way you think about your morning run.

Ruiz, D. (1997). *The four agreements: A practical guide to personal freedom.* Carlsbad, CA: Hay House.
Rooted in traditional Toltec wisdom beliefs, four agreements in life are essential steps on the path to personal freedom. As beliefs are transformed through maintaining these agreements, shamanic teacher and healer don Miguel Ruiz asserts lives will "become filled with grace, peace, and unconditional love."

Seidman, D. (2007). *How: Why how we do anything means everything—in business (and in life).* Hoboken, NJ: John Wiley.
It is no longer what you do that matters most and sets you apart from others but how you do what you do. This book explores how we think, how we behave, how we lead, and how we govern our institutions and ourselves to uncover the values-inspired "hows" of twenty-first-century

success and significance. The qualities that many once thought of as "soft"—values, trust, and reputation—are now the hard currency of success and the ultimate drivers of efficiency, performance, innovation, and growth. With in-depth insights and practical advice, *How* will help you bring excellence and significance to your business endeavors—and your life—and refocus your efforts in powerful new ways.

Sinek, S. (2009). *Start with why: How great leaders inspire everyone to take action*. New York, NY: Portfolio.

Why are some people and organizations more innovative, more influential, and more profitable than others? Why do some command greater loyalty? In studying the leaders who've had the greatest influence in the world, Simon Sinek discovered that they all think, act, and communicate in the exact same way—and it's the complete opposite of what everyone else does. People like Martin Luther King Jr., Steve Jobs, and the Wright brothers might have little in common, but they all started with *why*.

Sood, A., & Mayo Clinic. (2013). *The Mayo Clinic guide to stress-free living*. Cambridge, MA: Da Capo Press.

This is the Mayo Clinic's first book focusing on the urgent health issue of stress. Dr. Sood's program has two essential steps: the Basics and the Skills. In the Basics, readers come to understand the workings of the brain and what generates stress. Dr. Sood reveals insights about the mind's instinctive restlessness and shortsightedness that further increase stress and anxiety. The next step is the Skills, where readers learn how to enhance awareness, develop focus, and experience the present moment with greater joy. The result is lower stress.

Sutton, R. (2007). *The no asshole rule: Building a civilized workplace and surviving one that isn't*. New York, NY: Warner Business Books.

Sutton's book aims to show managers that hiring mean-spirited employees—regardless of talent—saps energy from everyone who must deal with said new hires. This idea is based on the notion, as adapted in hugely successful companies like Google and SAS, that employees with malicious intents or negative attitudes would destroy any sort of productive and pleasant working environment and hinder the entire operation's success.

Tarvis, C., & Aronson, E. (2007). *Mistakes were made (but not by me): Why we justify foolish beliefs, bad decisions, and hurtful acts*. Orlando, FL: Harcourt.

Why do people dodge responsibility when things fall apart? Why the parade of public figures unable to own up when they screw up? Why the endless marital quarrels over who is right? Why can we see hypocrisy in others but not in ourselves? Are we all liars? Or do we really believe the stories we tell? Backed by years of research and delivered in lively, energetic prose, *Mistakes Were Made (but Not by Me)* offers a fascinating explanation of self-deception—how it works, the harm it can cause, and how we can overcome it.

Tatum, B. (2003). *"Why are all the Black kids sitting together in the cafeteria?": And other conversations about race.* New York, NY: Basic Books.

Beverly Daniel Tatum, a renowned authority on the psychology of racism, asserts that we do not know how to talk about our racial differences: Whites are afraid of using the wrong words and being perceived as "racist," whereas parents of color are afraid of exposing their children to painful racial realities too soon. Using real-life examples and the latest research, Tatum presents strong evidence that straight talk about our racial identities—whatever they may be—is essential if we are serious about facilitating communication across racial and ethnic divides. We have waited far too long to begin our conversations about race.

Tull, A., Hirt, J., & Saunders, S. (2009). *Becoming socialized in student affairs administration: A guide for new professionals and their supervisors.* Sterling, VA: Stylus.

Effective socialization of new student affairs professionals is essential, both for the individual success of these practitioners and for the work of a college or university that promotes student learning. It enables new professionals to manage the important personal and professional transitions they experience throughout their careers, engage in continual professional development, and achieve high levels of productivity. It also counteracts the high attrition rate among new hires.

Watkins, M. (2003). *The first 90 days: Critical success strategies for new leaders at all levels.* Boston, MA: Harvard Business School Press.

Michael D. Watkins offers proven strategies for conquering the challenges of transitions—no matter where you are in your career. Watkins, a noted expert on leadership transitions and advisor to senior leaders in all types of organizations, also addresses today's increasingly demanding professional landscape, where managers face not only more frequent transitions but also steeper expectations once they step into their new jobs. You'll learn how to secure critical early wins, an important first step in establishing yourself in your new role.

Articles

McIntosh, P. (1988). *White privilege and male privilege: A personal account of coming to see correspondences through work in women's studies.* Wellesley, MA: Wellesley College Center for Research on Women.

American feminist and activist Peggy McIntosh explores the power of White privilege. How can people in positions of power dismantle the very systems that empower them? How can we become increasingly aware of our own privilege and the privilege (or lack thereof) of others? How do we transfer power to those who are different from us? These are some of the many questions that McIntosh inspires.

Whitt, E. J. (1997). "Don't drink the water?": A guide to encouraging a new institutional culture. In E. J. Whitt (Ed.), *College student affairs administration* (pp. 516–523). Needham Heights, MA: Simon & Schuster.

Whitt's article describes the process of transitioning to a new institutional culture and offers advice for learning about and developing an understanding and appreciation of their new organizational cultures.

Author

Sonja Ardoin is a learner, educator, and facilitator. She serves as the director of student leadership and engagement at the University of North Carolina Wilmington and instructs a few courses at the university. Originally from "Cajun country," Sonja began her higher education career as a first-generation college student at Louisiana State University where she earned a BS in secondary education. She moved on to Florida State University in 2005 to obtain her MS in higher education and student affairs and, after graduation, worked there full-time as an assistant director for student activities until 2008. Sonja's second role allowed her to serve as the class councils advisor for student activities at Texas A&M University from 2008 to 2010. Sonja then moved "north" to Raleigh to pursue her PhD in educational research and policy analysis, which she completed in May 2013 with a dissertation titled "Learning a Different Language: Rural Students' Comprehension of College Knowledge and University Jargon." Sonja currently volunteers with national organizations such as LeaderShape, Zeta Tau Alpha, and Lambda Chi Alpha and is an active member of NASPA and ACPA. Personally, Sonja enjoys spending time with loved ones, traveling, reading, dancing, exercising, and laughing.

Contributors

Raja Bhattar is a community organizer, speaker, and author and serves as the director of UCLA's Lesbian Gay Bisexual Transgender Campus Resource Center. He holds a master's degree from the University of Vermont and completed his bachelor's in psychology at Boston University. He has worked at the University of Vermont, Champlain College, and the University of Redlands in various administrative positions focusing on diversity and social justice initiatives. He has authored several articles and a national study of South Asian queer experiences on college campuses.

Robert "Bobby" Borgmann is the assistant director for programming at Florida International University, where he also earned his BA in English and

MS in higher education administration. Bobby started off in the Office of Campus Life as a coordinator in 2010, overseeing the Student Programming Council (SPC). In 2013, Bobby assumed his current role where he currently oversees homecoming and Week of Welcome and continues his work with SPC. He also contributes articles for the NACA *Campus Activities Programming* magazine and volunteers with the Sigma Alpha Mu fraternity.

Brandon Bowden is the associate director for research and programs in the Oglesby Union at Florida State University. He holds a master of science degree in higher education from Florida State University and is currently a doctoral candidate in the higher education department at Florida State University researching the impact of engagement on the persistence of minority students at predominantly White, public, four-year institutions. He also serves as an adjunct faculty member teaching Leadership and Change as part of the Undergraduate Certificate in Leadership studies at the university.

Jasmine P. Clay is the assistant director for Chadbourne Residential College at the University of Wisconsin–Madison. She earned an MS in student affairs and higher education from Indiana State University and is currently pursuing an EdD in educational leadership with a focus on higher education from Edgewood College in Madison, Wisconsin. Her research interests focus on the intersections of race and gender in the workplace and the impact of first-year and social justice seminar experiences on college students.

Kathy M. Collins is the director of residence education and housing services at Michigan State University (MSU). In this role she provides oversight and supervision to MSU's housing operations and the MSU Union. Prior to serving in this capacity, she was associate director of residence life at Texas A&M University. Kathy is the coeditor with Dr. Darby Roberts of *Learning Is Not a Sprint: Assessing and Documenting Student Leader Learning in Cocurricular Involvement* (2012). She has worked in many areas throughout student affairs including athletics, conduct, orientation, student activities, and housing and residence life. She earned her doctorate in higher education administration from Bowling Green State University, her master's degree in counseling with an emphasis in college student personnel administration from Shippensburg University in Pennsylvania, and her undergraduate degree in political science/international relations–business from Juniata College in Pennsylvania.

Allison Crume serves as the associate vice president for student affairs at Florida State University. She directly supervises Campus Recreation, University Health Services, University Housing, the Oglesby Union, and the

University Counseling Center. Her responsibilities also include the areas of finance and administration, assessment and research, and marketing and communications for the division. She also teaches as adjunct faculty in the department of educational leadership and policy studies. Allison, who earned a doctorate in higher education administration from Florida State University in 2004, also has experience in the areas of staff development, student activities, and policy development. Prior to Florida State University, Allison worked for the Board of Governors, State University System of Florida in the department of academic and student affairs. She is an active member of the National Association of Student Personnel Administrators (NASPA) and has served on its Region III board for several years. Her research interests include campus governance, women in higher education, professional development, and supervision. Her most joyful roles are as wife and mom.

Lindsey Katherine Dippold has more than 10 years of experience working in higher education with a specialization in career services. She is an adjunct faculty member in counseling within the Maricopa Community College District and an adjunct dissertation chair at NorthCentral University. Lindsey is currently serving as president-elect for the AzCPA, the Arizona state entity of the American College Personnel Association; is a board representative for AWHE, the Arizona Women in Higher Education Network; and is passionate about supporting students' success in college.

Amber Garrison Duncan is the evaluation and planning officer at Lumina Foundation, where she is responsible for designing and implementing the evaluation framework for the organization. Amber worked in student affairs for over 13 years, serving four different institutions in a variety of functional areas. In her last role she created the office of Student Affairs Assessment and Research at the University of Oregon. Amber's personal mission is to capture opportunities for change to bring about social good. She believes in the power of a postsecondary degree to empower individuals to create a better future for themselves and others.

Mat Erpelding serves in the Idaho House of Representatives and has worked in higher education for 19 years. In addition to teaching leadership and outdoor education, Mat is a high-altitude climbing guide and a business owner. Mat is a founder of SAGA Leadership Associates, which specializes in leadership development, group facilitation, and teaching collaboration using experiential education as its foundation. SAGA serves a variety of clients including the military, higher education institutions, and corporations who want to improve their organizational culture. He is an accomplished author and recently coedited *Outdoor Program Administration: Principles and Practices* (Association of Outdoor Recreation and Education, 2012). He earned an MA in adult education and organizational learning from the University of Idaho.

Jomita Fleming is currently an assistant director for residential life at Southern Methodist University in Dallas, Texas. She received her bachelor of science degree in psychology from Towson University and a master of arts in education from Virginia Polytechnic Institute and State University. She has also worked at American University and Texas A&M University. Nationally, she serves as a cochair for the Extended Orientation Network within the Association for Orientation, Transition and Retention in Higher Education and a colead facilitator for LeaderShape. She has served as a participant and intern for the Social Justice Training Institute and a core group facilitator for the Social Justice Training Institute: The Student Experience. Most important, she is a wife and the mom of two wonderful children, ages 6 and (almost) 2. She also serves on the parent-teacher association at her son's school.

Juan R. Guardia is assistant vice president for student affairs at Northeastern Illinois University in Chicago. Juan's work in education includes K–12 and higher education; he has been in the field of student affairs for more than 12 years in various administrative roles. Prior to his appointment at Northeastern Illinois University, he was the director of the Center for Multicultural Affairs and adjunct faculty in the higher education program at Florida State University. He earned his PhD in educational leadership–higher education administration from Iowa State University, a master's degree in higher education, a bachelor's degree in communication from Florida State University, and an associate in arts degree from Miami-Dade Community College.

Jordan Hale was born June 20, 1984, in Tallahassee, Florida. After graduating from college from the University of Florida in 2006 with a degree in history and economics, he attended the University of Massachusetts Amherst to pursue a master's degree in higher education administration. Upon graduation, Jordan took a job at Duke University in 2008 and still works at the institution as the director of New Student Programs. Jordan currently lives in Raleigh, North Carolina, with his wife, Tessa, and their awesome dog, Champ.

Sara Jones loves connecting people and ideas to each other and has been working in higher education alumni relations and development since 2004. She earned a master's in higher education administration from Florida State

University in 2006. She worked for multiple large public institutions before joining a nonprofit organization with responsibilities for coordinating educational programs for education-related advancement professionals.

T. J. Jourian is a higher education PhD student at Loyola University Chicago with particular interest in transmasculine and genderqueer students of color and critical social theories in higher education. He has experience in residence life, LGBTQI and multicultural affairs, and women's services and earned his MA in student affairs administration at Michigan State University. T. J. has conducted social-justice-themed trainings, workshops, and speaking engagements for more than a decade.

merz lim is the assistant director at the Asian American Cultural Center at Rutgers University–New Brunswick. merz began his student affairs career at Texas A&M University in 2008. He then pursued his MA in higher education in student affairs at the University of Connecticut working at the Asian American Cultural Center. He has also held a full-time position as the coordinator for Asian Pacific American Student Involvement and Advocacy at University of Maryland–College Park. He is involved with the ACPA Asian Pacific American Network (APAN) and the Asian Pacific Americans in Higher Education (APAHE) organizations.

Robert "Jason" Lynch was born and raised in Whiteville, North Carolina. He graduated from the University of North Carolina Wilmington in 2008 with degrees in biology and psychology, and in 2011, he obtained his master's degree in higher education administration. Currently, he works as a resident director in Unit 1 at the University of California, Berkeley.

becky martinez is a consultant with an emphasis on social justice, leadership, and organizational change. Her work focuses on dismantling systems of oppression through critical dialogue and reflection intertwined with theoretical foundations. She is currently a faculty member for the Social Justice Training Institute, a colead facilitator for the LeaderShape Institute, and a certified trainer with ADL and GLSEN. She holds a doctorate in organizational leadership, with her research centered on transformative learning, social justice, and racism, and prior to consultancy, she worked as a practitioner within the University of California, California State University, and Colorado State University systems, as well as private institutions.

Mary C. Medina started her higher education career at Clemson University, where she received a BA in mathematical sciences. She moved on to Florida

State University, where she obtained her MS in higher education with an emphasis in student affairs. Mary has worked professionally at Clemson University as the associate director of multicultural programs and services and at the University of Florida as the assistant director for employer development. She is currently a full-time PhD student in educational research and policy analysis, with a specialization in higher education administration, at North Carolina State University. She also has a graduate assistantship with NC State's Department of Multicultural Student Affairs. Mary is active in professional organizations such as the National Association of Student Personnel Administrators (NASPA) and Alpha Kappa Alpha Sorority, Incorporated.

Claudia Mercado serves as the associate vice chancellor for enrollment management at the City Colleges of Chicago, overseeing recruitment, retention, and completion initiatives for more than 110,000 students across a seven-campus system. Claudia has direct oversight of recruitment, admissions, advising, tutoring, first-year experience initiatives, and precollege programs. Prior to joining City Colleges of Chicago, Claudia served as the director of admissions at Northeastern Illinois University (NEIU), a Hispanic-serving institution, for four years, with direct oversight of recruitment and initiatives serving undocumented, LGBT, and other diverse students. Claudia had previously served as the assistant director of student activities at NEIU and oversaw Greek life, leadership programs, student media organizations, and assessment. Claudia began her career at the University of Kansas, serving as the associate director for multicultural recruitment in the Office of Admissions and Scholarships for six years. She also completed both master's and EdD degrees from the University of Kansas in higher education administration. She completed her bachelor of arts in English from Missouri State University. Claudia has served on multiple boards, including at Big Brothers Big Sisters, Dignity Chicago, and Sigma Alpha Chi Latina Sorority, and is a colead facilitator for LeaderShape. She resides in Chicago with her spouse and two young children.

Sandra Miles is the director of student affairs and university ombudsman at IUPUI–Columbus (IUPUC), where she oversees all student success services and serves as the chief diversity officer. She also teaches upper-division courses within the women's studies department. Sandra completed her doctoral work at Florida State University in 2012, earning a PhD in higher education administration. She completed her bachelor's degree and master's degree at the University of Central Florida. From 2005 to 2011, she worked at Florida State University as the assistant director of student activities and later the assistant director for student affairs–SGA advisor. She recently published a book chapter titled "'Bein' Alive & Bein' a Woman & Bein' Colored Is a Metaphysical Dilemma': Black Female Social Integration at a Predominantly White Institution" within the book *Support Systems and Services for Diverse Populations: Considering the Intersection of Race, Gender, and the Needs of Black Female Undergraduates* (*Diversity in Higher Education*, Vol. 8, Emerald Group, 2011). In addition to her career achievements, in the community Sandra is also the national director of the Black Female Development Circle, Inc., and is a member of the Indianapolis Alumnae Chapter of Delta Sigma Theta Sorority, Inc.

Laura Osteen is director of the Florida State University Center for Leadership and Social Change. The center is a campus-wide endeavor to transform lives through leadership education, identity development, and community engagement. As an adjunct professor in the College of Education's Higher Education and Leadership Program, Laura teaches in the university's undergraduate academic certificate/minor in leadership studies. She received her doctorate of philosophy degree from the University of Maryland in the field of college student personnel with an emphasis in leadership development and organizational change. Her master's degree is in student affairs and higher education from Colorado State University–Fort Collins, and her undergraduate degree is in speech communications from Indiana University–Bloomington.

Jeremiah Shinn serves as the assistant vice president for Student Life at Boise State University. Previously, he served in various student development roles at Boise State University, Indiana University, and Eastern Michigan University. Jeremiah is an active presenter and consultant on topics related to leadership, organizational development, and change management. He was the 2013 president of the Association of Fraternity/Sorority Advisors and has been an active volunteer for a number of projects and organizations dedicated to the development of student affairs professionals. He earned a master's degree in higher education and a doctoral degree in educational leadership.

Leisan C. Smith serves as the first director of the LGBTQ Center at her alma mater, the University of Cincinnati. In this role she oversees the day-to-day operations of the center; provides resources and support for LGBTQ students, staff, and faculty; and serves as an advocate for and designs and facilitates Safe Zone Training for the university and Cincinnati community. She also works as an adjunct faculty member at Northern Kentucky University teaching women and gender studies courses and is a member of Sigma Gamma Rho Sorority Inc. and MUSE, Cincinnati's Women's Choir (a feminist choir dedicated to musical excellence and social change).

Jackie C. Thomas Jr. currently serves as an assistant professor of education at Lone Star College–Tomball. His areas of research include academic motivation, persistence, and retention among minority college students. In his spare time, Jackie serves on the board of directors for the Foundation for Student Leadership and Success and is involved with Big Brothers Big Sisters and the LeaderShape Institute. He is also a proud member of Alpha Phi Alpha Fraternity, Inc. He received his bachelor of science in consumer science and merchandising from the University of Houston, his master of science in higher education from Florida State University, and his doctorate of philosophy in educational psychology and individual differences from the University of Houston.

Tanya O. Williams, deputy vice president for institutional diversity and community engagement at Union Theological Seminary in the city of New York, was born and raised in Houston and attended Texas A&M University for both her bachelor's degree (English and journalism) and her master's degree (higher education administration). After graduating with her master's degree in 1996, Tanya took a job at the University of Illinois, Urbana–Champaign, creating its first Intergroup Dialogue Program. She has also worked as director of diversity education at Southwestern University in Georgetown, Texas, and associate dean of students for diversity and inclusion at Mount Holyoke College in western Massachusetts. Tanya returned to school in 2001 to study social justice education at the University of Massachusetts, where she completed her doctorate researching internalized racism and a path to liberation for African Americans. She also is a senior trainer for the Class Action organization and a colead facilitator for the LeaderShape Institute.

MCGC. *See* Multicultural Greek
 Council
meaningfulness, 123
MEd. *See* master of education
meetings, for self-reflection, 131
Men of Color, 80
mentors, 24, 99
MGC. *See* Multicultural
 Greek Council
Miami-Dade Community College, 76
Miami University of Ohio, 5, 10
Michigan State University, 78
ministries, on campus, 16
mobility, 40
Molina, E., 27
MS. *See* master of science
multicultural affairs, 18
Multicultural Greek Council
 (MGC or MCGC), 17
multiracial students, 2
music, 128
Myers-Briggs Type Indicator
 (MBTI), 138

NACA. *See* National Association of
 Campus Activities
NALFO. *See* National Association of
 Latino Fraternal Organizations
NASPA. *See* National Association of
 Student Personnel Administrators
National Association of Campus
 Activities (NACA), 101, 116–17
National Association of Latino
 Fraternal Organizations
 (NALFO), 17, 78
National Association of Student
 Personnel Administrators
 (NASPA), 77, 80, 91–92, 96, 139
 career themes and, 25
 competency areas and, 30
 Region III Summer Symposium, 95
National Board of the Black Female
 Development Circle, Inc., 54
National Pan-Hellenic Conference
 (NPHC), 17

National Panhellenic Council (NPC), 17
networking, 106–7
 as career strategy, 37–38
 context for, 109
 personal stories on, 114–26
 politics and, 110–14
 style of, 109
 terminology for, 108
new professionals
 career themes for, 25–27
 competency areas for, 30–32
 defined, 20
 expectations and reality of, 21–25
 focus areas for, 29
 skills of, 27–29
New Zealand, 63
nontraditional students, 18
North Carolina State University, 5, 11
Northeastern Illinois University, 77
NPC. *See* National Panhellenic Council
NPHC. *See* National Pan-Hellenic
 Conference

Office of Diversity Programs
 and Services, 77
office politics, 38, 110
 departmental, 111
 divisional, 111–12
 with external partners, 113
 in the field, 113–14
 institutional, 112–13
online degree programs, 40–41
opportunities, for learning, 73–74
Order of the Eastern Star, 54
organizational resources, 31
orientation, 17–18
out group, 114
Owyang, Jeremiah, 106

parent-teacher organizations (PTA), 98
partners
 for collaboration, 112
 external, 113
part-time degree programs, 41–42
PD. *See* professional development

Demonstrating Student Success
A Practical Guide to Outcomes-Based Assessment of Learning and Development in Student Affairs
Marilee J. Bresciani, Megan Moore Gardner, and Jessica Hickmott

Transformative Learning Through Engagement
Student Affairs Practice as Experiential Pedagogy
Jane Fried and Associates
Foreword by James E. Zull

22883 Quicksilver Drive
Sterling, VA 20166-2102   Subscribe to our e-mail alerts: www.Styluspub.com

Resources for Student Affairs Professionals

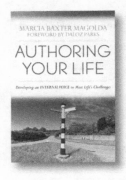

Authoring Your Life
Developing an Internal Voice to Navigate Life's Challenges
Marcia B. Baxter Magolda
Illustrated by Matthew Henry Hall
Foreword by Sharon Daloz Parks

Becoming Socialized in Student Affairs Administration
A Guide for New Professionals and Their Supervisors
Edited by Ashley Tull, Joan B. Hirt, and Sue Saunders

Contested Issues in Student Affairs
Diverse Perspectives and Respectful Dialogue
Edited by Peter M. Magolda and Marcia B. Baxter Magolda